GENETICS AND HEREDITY

THE HEALTHY BODY

Dale C. Garell, M.D. · General Editor

GENETICS AND HEREDITY

Edward Edelson

Introduction by C. Everett Koop, M.D., Sc.D.
former Surgeon General, U.S. Public Health Service

CHELSEA HOUSE PUBLISHERS

New York · Philadelphia

The goal of the ENCYCLOPEDIA OF HEALTH *is to provide general information in the ever-changing areas of physiology, psychology, and related medical issues. The titles in this series are not intended to take the place of the professional advice of a physician or other health care professional.*

ON THE COVER A computer model of DNA

Chelsea House Publishers
EDITOR-IN-CHIEF Remmel Nunn
MANAGING EDITOR Karyn Gullen Browne
COPY CHIEF Juliann Barbato
PICTURE EDITOR Adrian G. Allen
ART DIRECTOR Maria Epes
DEPUTY COPY CHIEF Mark Rifkin
ASSISTANT ART DIRECTOR Loraine Machlin
MANUFACTURING MANAGER Gerald Levine
SYSTEMS MANAGER Rachel Vigier
PRODUCTION MANAGER Joseph Romano
PRODUCTION COORDINATOR Marie Claire Cebrián

The Encyclopedia of Health
SENIOR EDITOR Paula Edelson

Staff for GENETICS AND HEREDITY
ASSISTANT EDITOR Nicole Bowen
COPY EDITOR Michael Goodman
EDITORIAL ASSISTANT Leigh Hope Wood
PICTURE RESEARCHER Georganne M. Backman
SENIOR DESIGNER Marjorie Zaum
DESIGN ASSISTANT Debora Smith

First Printing

1 3 5 7 9 8 6 4 2

Library of Congress Cataloging-in-Publication Data

Edelson, Edward
   Genetics and heredity / Edward Edelson.
     p. cm.—(The Encyclopedia of health)
   Includes bibliographical references.
   Summary: Discusses genetics from historical, medical, scientific, ethical, and practical viewpoints.
   ISBN 0-7910-0018-4
        0-7910-0458-9 (pbk.)
   1. Genetics. [1. Genetics.] I. Title. II. Series.   89-13994
QH430.E335 1990   CIP
575.1—dc20   AC

CONTENTS

THE ENCYCLOPEDIA OF
H E A L T H

THE HEALTHY BODY

The Circulatory System
Dental Health
The Digestive System
The Endocrine System
Exercise
Genetics & Heredity
The Human Body: An Overview
Hygiene
The Immune System
Memory & Learning
The Musculoskeletal System
The Neurological System
Nutrition
The Reproductive System
The Respiratory System
The Senses
Speech & Hearing
Sports Medicine
Vision
Vitamins & Minerals

THE LIFE CYCLE

Adolescence
Adulthood
Aging
Childhood
Death & Dying
The Family
Friendship & Love
Pregnancy & Birth

MEDICAL ISSUES

Careers in Health Care
Environmental Health
Folk Medicine
Health Care Delivery
Holistic Medicine
Medical Ethics
Medical Fakes & Frauds
Medical Technology
Medicine & the Law
Occupational Health
Public Health

PSYCHOLOGICAL DISORDERS AND THEIR TREATMENT

Anxiety & Phobias
Child Abuse
Compulsive Behavior
Delinquency & Criminal Behavior
Depression
Diagnosing & Treating Mental Illness
Eating Habits & Disorders
Learning Disabilities
Mental Retardation
Personality Disorders
Schizophrenia
Stress Management
Suicide

MEDICAL DISORDERS AND THEIR TREATMENT

AIDS
Allergies
Alzheimer's Disease
Arthritis
Birth Defects
Cancer
The Common Cold
Diabetes
First Aid & Emergency Medicine
Gynecological Disorders
Headaches
The Hospital
Kidney Disorders
Medical Diagnosis
The Mind-Body Connection
Mononucleosis and Other Infectious Diseases
Nuclear Medicine
Organ Transplants
Pain
Physical Handicaps
Poisons & Toxins
Prescription & OTC Drugs
Sexually Transmitted Diseases
Skin Disorders
Stroke & Heart Disease
Substance Abuse
Tropical Medicine

PREVENTION AND EDUCATION: THE KEYS TO GOOD HEALTH

C. Everett Koop, M.D., Sc.D.
former Surgeon General,
U.S. Public Health Service

The issue of health education has received particular attention in recent years because of the presence of AIDS in the news. But our response to this particular tragedy points up a number of broader issues that doctors, public health officials, educators, and the public face. In particular, it points up the necessity for sound health education for citizens of all ages.

Over the past 25 years this country has been able to bring about dramatic declines in the death rates for heart disease, stroke, accidents, and, for people under the age of 45, cancer. Today, Americans generally eat better and take better care of themselves than ever before. Thus, with the help of modern science and technology, they have a better chance of surviving serious—even catastrophic—illnesses. That's the good news.

But, like every phonograph record, there's a flip side, and one with special significance for young adults. According to a report issued in 1979 by Dr. Julius Richmond, my predecessor as Surgeon General, Americans aged 15 to 24 had a higher death rate in 1979 than they did 20 years earlier. The causes: violent death and injury, alcohol and drug abuse, unwanted pregnancies, and sexually transmitted diseases. Adolescents are particularly vulnerable because they are beginning to explore their own sexuality and perhaps to experiment with drugs. The need for educating young people is critical, and the price of neglect is high.

Yet even for the population as a whole, our health is still far from what it could be. Why? A 1974 Canadian government report attributed all death and disease to four broad elements: inadequacies in the health care system, behavioral factors or unhealthy life-styles, environmental hazards, and human biological factors.

To be sure, there are diseases that are still beyond the control of even our advanced medical knowledge and techniques. And despite yearnings that are as old as the human race itself, there is no "fountain of youth" to ward off aging and death. Still, there is a solution to many of the problems that undermine sound health. In a word, that solution is prevention. Prevention, which includes health promotion and education, saves lives, improves the quality of life, and, in the long run, saves money.

In the United States, organized public health activities and preventive medicine have a long history. Important milestones include the improvement of sanitary procedures and the development of pasteurized milk in the late 19th century, and the introduction in the mid-20th century of effective vaccines against polio, measles, German measles, mumps, and other once-rampant diseases. Internationally, organized public health efforts began on a wide-scale basis with the International Sanitary Conference of 1851, to which 12 nations sent representatives. The World Health Organization, founded in 1948, continues these efforts under the aegis of the United Nations, with particular emphasis on combatting communicable diseases and the training of health care workers.

Despite these accomplishments, much remains to be done in the field of prevention. For too long, we have had a medical care system that is science- and technology-based, focused, essentially, on illness and mortality. It is now patently obvious that both the social and the economic costs of such a system are becoming insupportable.

Implementing prevention—and its corollaries, health education and promotion—is the job of several groups of people.

First, the medical and scientific professions need to continue basic scientific research, and here we are making considerable progress. But increased concern with prevention will also have a decided impact on how primary care doctors practice medicine. With a shift to health-based rather than morbidity-based medicine, the role of the "new physician" will include a healthy dose of patient education.

Second, practitioners of the social and behavioral sciences—psychologists, economists, city planners—along with lawyers, business leaders, and government officials—must solve the practical and ethical dilemmas confronting us: poverty, crime, civil rights, literacy, education, employment, housing, sanitation, environmental protection, health care delivery systems, and so forth. All of these issues affect public health.

Third is the public at large. We'll consider that very important group in a moment.

Fourth, and the linchpin in this effort, is the public health profession—doctors, epidemiologists, teachers—who must harness the professional expertise of the first two groups and the common sense and cooperation of the third, the public. They must define the problems statistically and qualitatively and then help us set priorities for finding the solutions.

To a very large extent, improving those statistics is the responsibility of every individual. So let's consider more specifically what the role of the individual should be and why health education is so important to that role. First, and most obviously, individuals can protect themselves from illness and injury and thus minimize their need for professional medical care. They can eat nutritious food, get adequate exercise, avoid tobacco, alcohol, and drugs, and take prudent steps to avoid accidents. The proverbial "apple a day keeps the doctor away" is not so far from the truth, after all.

Second, individuals should actively participate in their own medical care. They should schedule regular medical and dental checkups. Should they develop an illness or injury, they should know when to treat themselves and when to seek professional help. To gain the maximum benefit from any medical treatment that they do require, individuals must become partners in that treatment. For instance, they should understand the effects and side effects of medications. I counsel young physicians that there is no such thing as too much information when talking with patients. But the corollary is the patient must know enough about the nuts and bolts of the healing process to understand what the doctor is telling him. That is at least partially the patient's responsibility.

Education is equally necessary for us to understand the ethical and public policy issues in health care today. Sometimes individuals will encounter these issues in making decisions about their own treatment or that of family members. Other citizens may encounter them as jurors in medical malpractice cases. But we all become involved, indirectly, when we elect our public officials, from school board members to the president. Should surrogate parenting be legal? To what extent is drug testing desirable, legal, or necessary? Should there be public funding for family planning, hospitals, various types of medical research, and medical care for the indigent? How should we allocate scant technological resources, such as kidney dialysis and organ transplants? What is the proper role of government in protecting the rights of patients?

What are the broad goals of public health in the United States today? In 1980, the Public Health Service issued a report aptly entitled *Promoting Health—Preventing Disease: Objectives for the Nation*. This report expressed its goals in terms of mortality and in terms of intermediate goals in education and health improvement. It identified 15 major concerns: controlling high blood pressure; improving family planning; improving pregnancy care and infant health; increasing the rate of immunization; controlling sexually transmitted diseases; controlling the presence of toxic agents and radiation in the environment; improving occupational safety and health; preventing accidents; promoting water fluoridation and dental health; controlling infectious diseases; decreasing smoking; decreasing alcohol and drug abuse; improving nutrition; promoting physical fitness and exercise; and controlling stress and violent behavior.

For healthy adolescents and young adults (ages 15 to 24), the specific goal was a 20% reduction in deaths, with a special focus on motor vehicle injuries and alcohol and drug abuse. For adults (ages 25 to 64), the aim was 25% fewer deaths, with a concentration on heart attacks, strokes, and cancers.

Smoking is perhaps the best example of how individual behavior can have a direct impact on health. Today cigarette smoking is recognized as the most important single preventable cause of death in our society. It is responsible for more cancers and more cancer deaths than any other known agent; is a prime risk factor for heart and blood vessel disease, chronic bronchitis, and emphysema; and is a frequent cause of complications in pregnancies and of babies born prematurely, underweight, or with potentially fatal respiratory and cardiovascular problems.

Since the release of the Surgeon General's first report on smoking in 1964, the proportion of adult smokers has declined substantially, from 43% in 1965 to 30.5% in 1985. Since 1965, 37 million people have quit smoking. Although there is still much work to be done if we are to become a "smoke-free society," it is heartening to note that public health and public education efforts—such as warnings on cigarette packages and bans on broadcast advertising—have already had significant effects.

In 1835, Alexis de Tocqueville, a French visitor to America, wrote, "In America the passion for physical well-being is general." Today, as then, health and fitness are front-page items. But with the greater scientific and technological resources now available to us, we are in a far stronger position to make good health care available to everyone. And with the greater technological threats to us as we approach the 21st century, the need to do so is more urgent than ever before. Comprehensive information about basic biology, preventive medicine, medical and surgical treatments, and related ethical and public policy issues can help you arm yourself with the knowledge you need to be healthy throughout your life.

FOREWORD

Dale C. Garell, M.D.

Advances in our understanding of health and disease during the 20th century have been truly remarkable. Indeed, it could be argued that modern health care is one of the greatest accomplishments in all of human history. In the early 1900s, improvements in sanitation, water treatment, and sewage disposal reduced death rates and increased longevity. Previously untreatable illnesses can now be managed with antibiotics, immunizations, and modern surgical techniques. Discoveries in the fields of immunology, genetic diagnosis, and organ transplantation are revolutionizing the prevention and treatment of disease. Modern medicine is even making inroads against cancer and heart disease, two of the leading causes of death in the United States.

Although there is much to be proud of, medicine continues to face enormous challenges. Science has vanquished diseases such as smallpox and polio, but new killers, most notably AIDS, confront us. Moreover, we now victimize ourselves with what some have called "diseases of choice," or those brought on by drug and alcohol abuse, bad eating habits, and mismanagement of the stresses and strains of contemporary life. The very technology that is doing so much to prolong life has brought with it previously unimaginable ethical dilemmas related to issues of death and dying. The rising cost of health care is a matter of central concern to us all. And violence in the form of automobile accidents, homicide, and suicide remains the major killer of young adults.

In the past, most people were content to leave health care and medical treatment in the hands of professionals. But since the 1960s, the consumer of medical care—that is, the patient—has assumed an increasingly central role in the management of his or her own health. There has also been a new emphasis placed on prevention: People are recognizing that their own actions can help prevent many of the conditions that have caused death and disease in the past. This accounts for the growing commitment to good nutrition and regular exercise, for the fact that more and more people are choosing not to smoke, and for a new moderation in people's drinking habits.

People want to know more about themselves and their own health. They are curious about their body: its anatomy, physiology, and biochemistry. They want to keep up with rapidly evolving medical technologies and procedures. They are willing to educate themselves about common disorders and diseases so that they can be full partners in their own health care.

The ENCYCLOPEDIA OF HEALTH is designed to provide the basic knowledge that readers will need if they are to take significant responsibility for their own health. It is also meant to serve as a frame of reference for further study and exploration. The ENCYCLOPEDIA is divided into five subsections: The Healthy Body; the Life Cycle; Medical Disorders & Their Treatment; Psychological Disorders & Their Treatment; and Medical Issues. For each topic covered by the ENCYCLOPEDIA, we present the essential facts about the relevant biology; the symptoms, diagnosis, and treatment of common diseases and disorders; and ways in which you can prevent or reduce the severity of health problems when that is possible. The ENCYCLOPEDIA also projects what may lie ahead in the way of future treatment or prevention strategies.

The broad range of topics and issues covered in the ENCYCLOPEDIA reflects the fact that human health encompasses physical, psychological, social, environmental, and spiritual well-being. Just as the mind and the body are inextricably linked, so, too, is the individual an integral part of the wider world that comprises his or her family, society, and environment. To discuss health in its broadest aspect it is necessary to explore the many ways in which it is connected to such fields as law, social science, public policy, economics, and even religion. And so, the ENCYCLOPEDIA is meant to be a bridge between science, medical technology, the world at large, and you. I hope that it will inspire you to pursue in greater depth particular areas of interest and that you will take advantage of the suggestions for further reading and the lists of resources and organizations that can provide additional information.

CHAPTER 1

BEGINNINGS

The mysteries of heredity have always fascinated scientists. The process by which one generation gives rise to the next, with offspring basically resembling parents yet somehow different, has been a continuing source of wonder and speculation. Well before they understood the process, humans were able to manipulate it, breeding horses for speed, cattle for meat or milk, plants for beauty or yield. Yet in 1872, Charles Darwin, who provided the first good explanation of how species evolve, wrote:

> The laws governing inheritance are for the most part unknown. No one can say why the same peculiarity in different individuals of the same species, or in different species, is sometimes inherited and sometimes not so; why the child often reverts in certain characteristics to its grandfather or grandmother or remote ancestor.

Darwin's ideas sparked an intense interest in heredity and the inquiry into how species inherit and pass along certain traits.

DARWIN AND EVOLUTION

Charles Darwin's development of the theory of evolution through *natural selection*—the "survival of the fittest"—is probably one of the most familiar scientific stories. Although most people would claim to know what the theory of evolution is, many have only the vague idea that people descended from monkeys and may know more of the myth of Darwin's discovery than of the reality.

Darwin was born in 1809 to Robert Waring Darwin, an English doctor, and Susannah Wedgwood, an heir of Josiah Wedgwood, the ceramic ware manufacturer. He studied natural science at Cambridge University and, in December of 1831, set sail for the Pacific Coast of South America and nearby islands aboard the HMS *Beagle*. Darwin's time on the *Beagle* allowed him the leisure to read and to think through various theories and ideas on evolution. It also gave him the unique opportunity to study the species of flora and fauna native to these regions. Among the creatures Darwin made famous were the many species of finches he encountered on the Galápagos Islands.

Although exact accounts, including Darwin's own writings and notebooks, vary, Darwin developed his theory of the evolution of species through natural selection using the data gathered on this voyage. Briefly, Darwin's theory is that evolution occurs in response to the competition for food that results because there are more animals than there is food for them. (Darwin based this idea on Thomas Malthus's theory in *An Essay on the Principle of Population* [1798] that human populations increase geometrically, whereas the food supply increases only arithmetically. He further supported it with direct observation of nature.) By chance of nature, some animals will have slight variations from other animals. The variations that allow them to acquire food more easily or more quickly give these animals a better chance of reproducing, thereby passing on their adaptations to their offspring. Eventually, a new species is developed.

Darwinian evolution pitted individual animals of a species, not groups of animals, against other individual animals of the same species in a competition to reproduce. "Survival of the fittest" refers to the ability to reproduce, not, as is often believed, to the ability to be the strongest, smartest, fastest, or most beautiful. Darwin's belief that each species evolved from a preexisting species was extremely controversial. In the mid-19th century, most people in Europe and America believed that humans were created by God, not, as Darwin's revolutionary proposal suggested, descended from a lower animal species. Many people felt that to suggest such an idea was blasphemous.

Controversy over the theory of evolution has continued since Darwin first proposed it (in a joint paper with Alfred Russel

In 1858, Charles Darwin proposed his theory of the evolution of species through natural selection. This principle became the basis for the modern study of genetics and evolution.

Wallace [1823–1913], who had simultaneously come up with the same theory) before the Linnaean Society of London in 1858. In the late 1800s, scientists seeking to refute Darwin's theory of natural selection resurrected, in a somewhat altered form, the ideas of Jean-Baptiste Lamarck (1744–1829). Lamarckism claimed that animals developed certain characteristics in response to a perceived need (for example, giraffes developed a longer neck when they needed to eat leaves high in trees). It was proposed that these favorable *acquired characteristics* were passed on to offspring. These ideas were disproved, but the battle surrounding evolution continued.

In 1925, a schoolteacher from Dayton, Tennessee, was tried for teaching Darwin's theory of evolution. The trial gained nationwide attention; attorney Clarence Darrow's defense of the teacher John Scopes became known as a defense of evolution. Scopes lost the case but was later released on a technicality. The controversy over evolution continues to the present day despite solid scientific evidence supporting the theory.

Today many of the mysteries of heredity have been solved. Scientists not only understand the basic mechanisms of inheritance but are also increasingly able to duplicate them in the laboratory. There still is not a full answer to the issues posed by Charles Darwin, but scientists are well on the way toward that achievement.

GENETICS OF CELLS

The road to the modern field of *genetics* resulted from the merging of two pathways. One began in the 17th century, when scientists began using the microscope to examine the structure of living things. In England in the late 17th century, Robert Hooke (1635–1703) looked at slices of cork under a microscope and saw a mass of tiny compartments he called *cells*. Over the next century and more, other observers saw similar cells in other plant tissue and in animal tissue and established that the cell was the basic unit of living organisms. In the 1860s, the German pathologist Rudolf Virchow pronounced a principle that soon was accepted: All cells come from cells.

What most 19th-century biologists saw through the microscope was a cell consisting of a wall filled with a misty fluid they called protoplasm, or *cytoplasm*. In the cytoplasm was a small body called the *nucleus*; most other details of cell structure were unclear until better microscopes were developed.

Details began to emerge in the 1880s, when the German biologist Walther Flemming made a series of observations of cells that had been stained with red dyes. The dyes brought out previously unseen structures in the cell, and Flemming was able to describe the process by which a cell reproduces itself by dividing in two. Through the microscope, Flemming could see a dye-absorbing material in the cell nucleus. He called the nuclear material *chromatin*, from the Greek word for "color." When the cell began to divide, the chromatin drew up in threads. The wall around the nucleus dissolved, and the chromatin threads divided, half going to each end of the cell. The cell then divided in two, a nucleus appeared in each of the two cells, and the chromatin broke up into granules. The threads appeared again at the time of the next cell division, when the process was repeated. Flemming called the whole process *mitosis*, after the Greek word for "thread." The threads of chromatin seen by Flemming were named *chromosomes*, Greek for "colored bodies," by a German anatomist, Wilhelm von Waldeyer.

Biologists began observing mitosis in cells from a number of species, animal and plant, and soon found that each species had a fixed number of chromosomes. It seemed obvious that chromosomes had a role in heredity; a few bold biologists hypothesized that they were the means by which traits were passed from parents to offspring. That hypothesis gained support from a theory proposed by the German biologist August Weismann and proved by a Belgian, Edouard van Beneden. If chromosomes were the carriers of traits from generation to generation, Weismann said, then each human parent would contribute half an offspring's chromosomes. Therefore, the sex cells—a *sperm* cell from the father, an egg cell, or ovum, from the mother—would each carry only half the number of chromosomes seen in ordinary cells; the combination of ovum and sperm would form a cell with a full complement of chromosomes. Van Beneden's observations bore out that prediction. In ordinary cell division, the number of chromosomes doubles, with one complete set going to each new cell. Chromosome number does not double in the cell di-

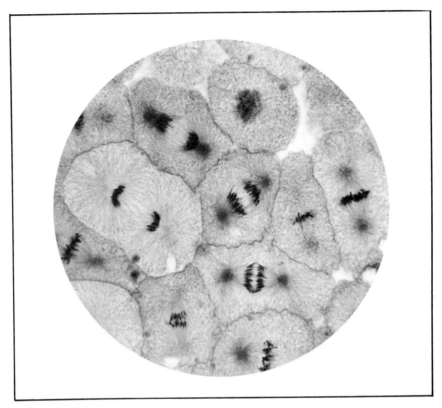

A microphotograph shows whitefish cells going through the various stages of mitosis. In some cells, the chromosomes, dark threadlike structures, are just beginning to pull apart; other cells exhibit two nuclei and show the start of the division of the cytoplasm.

vision that produces sperm and eggs, so each sperm or egg gets half the full complement of chromosomes. This kind of cell division is called *meiosis*, from the Greek for "to diminish."

By the end of the 19th century, work in *cytology* (the study of cells) pointed toward a theory of inheritance that involved passage of particles, the chromosomes, from parent to offspring. The next major advance came, in a most unexpected way, from an entirely different field—the study of hybrid plants.

HEREDITY

Three scientists in three countries—Hugo de Vries of Holland, Karl Correns of Germany, and Erich von Tschermak of Austria—had been trying to determine the laws of heredity by doing experiments with plants. All three came to essentially the same conclusion at about the same time, in the year 1900. As they prepared to publish their results, all three found they had been anticipated by an unknown monk whose report had lain unnoticed in an obscure journal for more than three decades. When their report was published, the three scientists gave credit to the original discoverer, Gregor Mendel (1822–84), who has since been regarded as the author of the laws of genetics.

Mendel's Experiments

Mendel's stroke of genius was to clarify the issue of heredity by looking at one trait at a time. Other researchers and theorists studying heredity had confused the issue by trying to explain everything at once. Working in his monastery garden, Mendel used different varieties of peas to look at the inheritance of one trait at a time: seed color (yellow or green); seed shape (smooth or wrinkled); stem size (long or short).

In one set of experiments, Mendel *crossed* (bred together different strains or species) long-stemmed and short-stemmed pea plants. All the offspring had long stems. When Mendel took these plants and crossed them again, the resulting generation included plants with both long and short stems. Mendel did the same kind of experiment with strains of peas that had either smooth seeds or wrinkled seeds and got similar results. All the plants in the first generation had smooth seeds. In the second generation, some plants had smooth seeds; some had wrinkled seeds.

Mendel then performed one of the essential operations of science: He counted. The count showed a *definite ratio* (a fixed quantitative relationship) in the second-generation plants for each characteristic: 75% to 25%. That is, there were three plants with long stems to every plant with a short stem and three smooth-seeded plants for every one with wrinkled seeds.

So two mysteries had to be explained. How could a trait disappear in one generation and appear again in the next? Why did these traits occur in a three-to-one ratio?

Mendel's paper explained the results of his experiments. Each trait—such as stem length and seed texture—is governed by a pair of hereditary factors transmitted from parents to offspring. One of the two factors for each trait is more powerful than the other—the factor for a long stem, for example, and the factor for smoothness. In the first generation, these factors masked the existence of the factors for short stems and wrinkles. But the factors for short stems and wrinkles were still present and made themselves visible in the next generation.

It was the arithmetic of the study, Mendel went on, that indicated that each trait was governed by two factors, one inherited from each parent. In the first generation, each plant inherited one strong factor and one weak one, so only the trait governed by the strong factor was visible—long stems in one experiment, smooth seeds in the other. But in the second generation, if one assumed that each factor was inherited independently of the other, one-quarter of the plants would inherit two strong factors; they would have long stems (or smooth seeds). Half would inherit one strong and one weak factor; they also would have long stems. One-quarter would inherit two weak factors and would have short stems.

The language scientists use has changed, and later experiments have significantly altered and expanded Mendel's explanation. Scientists now call hereditary factors *genes*; they refer to the strong factors as *dominant*, the weak factors as *recessive*. (The British biologist William Bateson [1861–1926] coined the term *genetics* in 1902.) Genes are not always completely dominant or recessive; in some cases they can compromise to produce intermediate characteristics. Also, in some cases there are more than two possible factors; instead of either long or short stems, a factor might produce, for example, fur of black, brown, gray, or white on a mouse. Only two factors would act in any given cross, but those two would have come from a possible four. Otherwise, as de Vries, Correns, and von Tschermak could testify in 1900 and as others would today, Mendel's work has stood the test of time.

Later Experiments

Bateson's experiments were the first to modify the Mendelian rules. Instead of looking at just one trait, Bateson looked at the simultaneous inheritance of two—flower color and pollen-grain shape—in sweet peas. Following the inheritance of these traits through a number of generations, Bateson found that they were

Gregor Mendel performed genetic experiments with pea plants in his monastery garden. He studied the inheritance of one trait at a time and discovered that traits were governed by strong and weak factors and were inherited in a ratio of three to one.

not transmitted independently. He accepted the idea that each trait was governed by a different gene but noted, "There is evidence of a linking or coupling between distinct characters."

In 1904, the American scientist Walter Sutton (1877–1916), a student at Columbia University, noted that the chromosomes seemed to meet the description of the hereditary factors Mendel had postulated. An offspring received two sets of chromosomes, one from each parent cell, so it seemed logical that they carried the genetic information. The only problem with that notion was that there were very few chromosomes and many, many traits. Rather than the chromosomes being the genes, it seemed more logical to assume that they were packages that contained the genes.

Drosophila

One young American scientist, Thomas Hunt Morgan (1866–1945) of Columbia University, was not convinced that Mendel and Bateson had the right explanation. Seeking a better set of rules to explain inheritance, he chose to work with a small fly, *Drosophila melanogaster* (commonly referred to as a fruit fly, although it is actually a pomace fly). The fruit fly has a number of advantages. It breeds quickly and in abundance, can be raised easily, requires little food, and does not take up much space. With four pairs of chromosomes, *Drosophila* has just enough complexity to make it interesting. It still is a standard tool for genetic research.

Morgan's first experiments were unrewarding. According to a now-classic story, the breakthrough came when his wife spotted an unusual white-eyed fly—*Drosophila* normally has red eyes—on a laboratory bench. The mutant, a male, was captured and bred to a normal red-eyed female. All the offspring in the first generation had red eyes, whereas 75% of those in the second generation had red eyes, 25% white eyes—the 3-to-1 Mendelian ratio. But there was a major oddity: All the white-eyed flies were males. In later generations, it was possible to produce some white-eyed females through crossbreeding, but all the males in the crossbreeding sample had white eyes.

Morgan traced the unusual finding to a difference between the chromosomes of male and female *Drosophila*. The females had four identical pairs of chromosomes. The males had only three identical pairs. The fourth pair consisted of a full-sized chromosome, called the *X chromosome* because of its shape, and a much smaller one, called the *Y chromosome*. The sex of a fly was clearly related to that fourth pair of chromosomes. A female had two X chromosomes; a male had an X and a Y. Something about the Y chromosome determined maleness.

But Morgan was forced to conclude that something about the Y also determined eye color in *Drosophila*. The gene for red eyes was clearly dominant. Assuming it was on the X chromosome, the first generation consisted of XX red-eyed females and XY red-eyed males. In that generation, the females produce eggs that all carry the X chromosome. The males produce sperm that contain either X or Y chromosomes. The XX female offspring all have red eyes; the XY males all have white eyes. Morgan followed his data and concluded that Mendel's rules were right and that chromosomes indeed are the carriers of genetic traits.

That was only the first of his discoveries. In a long series of experiments, Morgan identified a number of traits linked with sex chromosomes. But the inheritance pattern of some traits was not as simple as one would assume from previous studies. Following generation after generation of *Drosophila*, Morgan found anomalies. For example, in eye color studies he found an occasional white-eyed female or red-eyed male. Other traits that normally were linked were sometimes found to separate. After long analysis, Morgan and his colleagues explained these unusual occurrences as flaws in the way chromosomes reproduce and distribute themselves in offspring cells.

One of Morgan's students, Calvin Bridges (1889–1938), detected one kind of mistake when he looked at the cells of red-eyed males and white-eyed females. In these cells, something had gone wrong with the distribution of chromosomes. The white-eyed females had two X chromosomes and one Y; the red-eyed males had one X chromosome and no Y. They were the products of sex cells in which meiosis had not gone as it usually did.

Another kind of "mistake" was found in studies of other traits— a kind of mistake that helped explain Bateson's finding. Morgan showed that some traits did tend to go together but that sometimes their linkage changed. That traits went together indicated that their genes were on the same chromosomes, presumably part of a long chain. That the linkage could change indicated that occasionally, in the process of reproduction, the chain broke and two genes for different traits were separated. This process is called *crossing-over* because the broken end of one half of a chromosome usually crosses over and joins the other half, often resulting in an exchange of material. Crossing-over was found to provide a powerful tool for studying genes. By observing how often two traits are separated, it was possible to estimate how close together their genes are on a chromosome. Thus, it was possible to start making a genetic map of *Drosophila melanogaster*—and of other species, including humans.

Such mistakes of nature have turned out to be of major importance in the study of genetics. Biologists have been able to learn a great deal by examining genetic mistakes—how they occur, what they do, how they are inherited. In particular, biologists study *mutations*, permanent transmissible changes in a gene. When Morgan began his work, he had to rely on natural mutations, such as the one for white eyes. A number of methods for increasing the mutation rate were tried, but none worked. Then one of Morgan's students, Hermann Joseph Muller (1890– 1967), found that the frequency of mutations could be amazingly increased by exposing *Drosophila* to *X rays* (electromagnetic radiation of an extremely short wavelength). Morgan was awarded the 1933 Nobel Prize in physiology or medicine for his work in genetics; later, in 1946, Muller won the same Nobel Prize for showing how to make mutations.

So by 1930, biologists had a good foundation for understanding the transmission of traits. But there was a lot they did not know. What was a gene? What did it do? How did it mutate? The answers soon began to emerge.

•   •   •   •

CHAPTER 2

GENES AND
NUCLEIC ACIDS

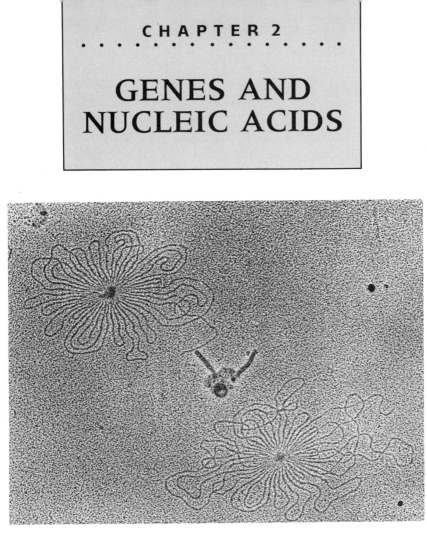

DNA from 2 bacteriophages magnified 100,000 times

Two major questions faced biologists at the start of the 1930s: What does a gene do? and What is a gene made of? The first question was answered in the 1930s, the second in the 1940s. The answers laid the foundation for today's era of *molecular biology*, which explains the traits of living organisms in terms of the behavior of their *molecules* (the combination of two or more atoms—the smallest unit of an element that can exist—to form a specific substance).

To understand molecular biology, one must be familiar with some basic organic chemistry. Organic biochemicals, the chemicals in living things, tend to be very large. Many of them are giant chains whose links are simpler molecules. For example, *carbohydrates* are chains of molecules called *sugars*. The simplest carbohydrates consist of just one or two sugar units. The largest consist of hundreds or thousands. Plants are mainly composed of carbohydrates.

Animals, on the other hand, are mainly composed of a different kind of giant molecule, a *protein*. Hair and skin, for example, are mostly protein. A protein is a chain whose subunits are *amino acids*, so named because they behave chemically as acids and contain amine groups, which are derived from ammonia. (Officially, a protein is a large chain of amino acids or two or more linked chains. A small chain is called a *polypeptide* because the link between amino acids is called a *peptide bond*. Proteins consist of several polypeptides.) There are 20 different amino acids from which human proteins are directly synthesized.

Living cells contain an enormous variety of proteins called *enzymes*, which carry out the basic functions of the cell. Many enzymes are *catalysts*, meaning that they speed up a chemical reaction. The chemical reactions that enable a cell to function and reproduce all depend on enzymes.

All of these facts were known in the 1930s when George W. Beadle and Edward L. Tatum began a series of experiments at Stanford University to learn what genes do. Beadle had started working with *Drosophila* but gave it up in favor of a much simpler organism called *Neurospora crassa*, a single-cell mold that sometimes grows on wet bread. *Neurospora* is not only easier to manage than is *Drosophila*, but it also has only a single set of seven chromosomes, making it simpler for geneticists to deal with.

Beadle and Tatum first bombarded *Neurospora* with X rays to obtain mutations. Then they mated the mutated molds with normal ones and placed the *spores* (primitive, usually unicellular reproductive bodies) that resulted from the matings in petri dishes that contained the basic supply of the food they needed. Most of the colonies grew, but some did not. In those colonies that did not grow, the mutation had changed the mold's nutritional requirements. Beadle and Tatum began adding supplements to see what was missing. They found a variety of supplements that made the mutated spores start growing. One was a *vitamin* (one of various organic substances essential in minute amounts to most plants and animals), vitamin B_6, another was vitamin B_1, a third was the amino acid called *arginine.*

In this mutant, the X rays apparently had destroyed a gene that allowed *Neurospora* to make arginine. In a series of experiments, Beadle and Tatum were able to show that more than one gene was involved. Instead of adding arginine, they added various molecules that the normal cell could use to manufacture arginine. Different mutants required different precursor molecules to manufacture arginine. Beadle and Tatum were able to show that there is a chain of biochemical reactions, each catalyzed by a different enzyme, that starts with a beginning molecule and ends with production of arginine. Destroy any enzyme in that chain and arginine production is stopped.

Beadle and Tatum had established what genes do. They make enzymes. Each gene codes for one particular enzyme: one gene, one enzyme. The discovery won them the Nobel Prize for physiology or medicine in 1958 (shared with Joshua Lederberg).

NUCLEIC ACIDS

Once it was known that each gene coded for a protein, the next question was, What are genes made of? In the 1930s, the leading candidate was protein. That was wrong. It is now known that the genetic material is another giant molecule called *nucleic acid.* It was an understandable mistake, though. Proteins are very complex molecules, so it seemed likely that they could transmit the complicated messages needed to govern traits. Nucleic acid, by contrast, seemed simple—too simple to contain a complex message.

Nucleic acid was discovered in the 1860s by Johann Friedrich Miescher, a Swiss scientist working in Germany. Miescher wanted to study the cell nucleus. He chose to work with pus because it was known that the nucleus of the pus cell was unusually large. Miescher gathered pus from hospital bandages, broke down the cells with *pepsin* (a digestive enzyme), and after various chemical treatments obtained a fine white powder that was neither protein nor carbohydrate and contained a lot of was neither protein nor carbohydrate and contained a lot of *phosphorus* (a chemical element). Miescher named the material nuclein; his student Richard Altmann, who purified it, later re-named it nucleic acid.

It was not until some 40 years later that the composition of nucleic acid was determined. A German chemist, Albrecht Kos-sel, found that it included sugar, phosphate groups, and four nitrogen-containing compounds, or *nitrogenous bases*: *adenine* and *guanine*, which are called *purines*, and *thymine* and *cytosine*, which are called *pyrimidines*. (These nitrogenous bases are ab-breviated, respectively, as A, G, T, and C.) And, although the complete molecule is an acid, those four components are bases. (A base is the chemical opposite of an acid.) A Russian-born American scientist, Phoebus A. T. Levene, reported that the sug-ars in nucleic acid are different. Most sugar molecules contain six carbon atoms; the ones in nucleic acid contain five. Levene found two different sugars in nucleic acid; one type had one fewer oxygen atom than the other. He discovered the first in 1909; but the second, not until 1929. He named one sugar *ribose* and the other one *deoxyribose*. Thus, there were two nucleic acids— *ribonucleic acid*, or RNA, and *deoxyribonucleic acid*, or DNA.

Other differences between RNA and DNA were noted. Both contained adenine, guanine, and cytosine, but RNA contained the pyrimidine called *uracil* (U) instead of thymine. Sometime later, it was learned that DNA is found largely in the cell nucleus and RNA is found largely outside the nucleus.

The basic subunit of a nucleic acid consists of a sugar joined to a phosphate group and a base. It is called a *nucleotide*. A nucleic acid consists of a long chain of nucleotides, just as a protein consists of a chain of amino acids. But whereas any 1 of 20 amino acids can occupy 1 location in the protein chain, giving the possibility of enormous variety and complexity, the nucleic acid chain seems much simpler, with only 4 nucleotides forming its links. This simplicity made most researchers believe that nu-cleic acid could not encode the immense amount of information that genes carry. In addition, Levene had proposed that the basic unit of a nucleic acid consisted of all four nitrogenous bases linked together, repeated again and again (e.g., GACT, GACT, etc.)—a very dull molecule, indeed.

The research that changed that view began in the 1920s when Fred Griffith, a medical officer in the British Ministry of Health, began studying the family of *bacteria* (unicellular organisms that lack a distinct nuclear membrane) called pneumococci. Griffith compared the pneumococci that cause pneumonia with pneumococci that cause no disease. One difference was that the virulent pneumococci formed colonies with smooth surfaces when grown in the laboratory, whereas the harmless kind formed colonies with rough surfaces. In his key experiment, Griffith killed smooth pneumococci with steam and injected the dead bacteria into mice along with live rough pneumococci.

The mice died of pneumonia. In his postmortem examination, Griffith found their blood filled with the virulent, smooth strain. Griffith concluded that the rough bacteria had broken up in the bodies of the mice and had been used as food to rebuild the smooth pneumococci, a result he published in 1928.

Griffith was wrong. In fact, what had happened was that something in the smooth bacteria had transformed the rough bacteria

Scientists working with pneumococci (shown below magnified 1,000 times) discovered that the genetic material of these bacteria was DNA. Later studies showed this to be the genetic material of all living organisms.

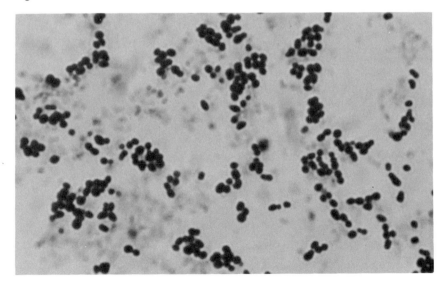

into smooth bacteria. That something was the genetic material. But Griffith's experiment provided a clue that was picked up by several scientists at the Rockefeller Institute Hospital (now Rockefeller University). The crucial experiments were done in the 1940s by Oswald T. Avery, working with Colin M. MacLeod and Maclyn McCarty. Using techniques developed at the institute, they broke the smooth bacteria apart and tested various components to see whether they would transform the rough bacteria.

When the components were exposed to enzymes that break down protein, the transformation still occurred. Therefore, the transforming factor was not protein. When the carbohydrates that make the bacteria look smooth were broken down by enzymes, the transformation again occurred; the transforming factor was not carbohydrate. But exposure to enzymes that break down nucleic acid stopped the transformation. The transforming factor was nucleic acid—specifically, tests showed, DNA. Thus, DNA was the genetic material of the pneumococcus bacteria. The three researchers published their results in 1944. Other scientists followed up Avery's report with experiments demonstrating that DNA was the genetic material of all the organisms they tested.

Discovering the Double Helix

The identification of DNA as primary genetic material raised a new question: How does DNA carry the information needed to govern the incredibly complex organization and activity of living organisms?

The first step was to discard Levene's concept of DNA as an unvaried molecule. If his theory were right, all four nucleotides would be present in equal amounts in all nucleic acids. Studies by Erwin Chargaff and Ernst Vischer at Columbia University showed this was not so. The content of various nucleotides varied greatly in samples of DNA from different species. But Chargaff and Vischer noted one constant. Any DNA sample had equal amounts of guanine and cytosine, and the number of adenines always equaled the number of thymines.

Then, in the early 1950s, a race began to put these bits of information together into a coherent picture of the structure and function of DNA. Several teams were working on the problem, but the race was believed to be between James D. Watson, an American, and Francis H. C. Crick, working at Cambridge University in England; and Linus Pauling and Robert B. Corey, working in the United States at the California Institute of Technology.

Pauling and his colleagues had just used a method called *X-ray crystallography* to determine the structure of proteins. In X-ray crystallography, the scientist directs a beam of X rays at a very pure sample—a *crystal* (a substance with an endlessly repeated structural unit in a perfectly regular pattern)—of the molecules being studied. By studying the way the X rays are deflected by atoms (the smallest unit an element can be reduced to and still retain its distinctive properties) in the crystal, it is possible to deduce the structure of the molecules. Pauling and Corey had found that many proteins are shaped like a coil, or *helix*. They believed DNA had a similar structure. They presented their ideas on the structure of DNA in the February 1953 issue of the *Proceedings of the National Academy of Sciences*. The article proposed that DNA was a helix but that it was a triple helix with the phosphate groups inside and the bases radiating out.

A British colleague of Crick's, Maurice H. F. Wilkins, worked along similar lines, using X-ray crystallography work done by his associate, Rosalind Franklin, who died of cancer at a tragically young age in 1958. The X-ray patterns showed DNA with a regular, repeating structure with a helical shape. But the exact nature of the helix remained unclear. Franklin's skills in X-ray crystallography enabled her to develop the idea of a model with a double helix, the phosphate-sugar backbone on the outside and the bases on the inside. She presented it in 1951 at a talk, attended by Watson, at Cambridge. Watson apparently did not remember or accept this; he and Crick pursued a triple helix for a time after that. Franklin herself was thrown off course by what seemed to be contradictions in her X-ray photographs. Animosity between Franklin and Wilkins also slowed their progress.

Watson and Crick came up with the right solution first. They published it in the April 25, 1953, issue of *Nature*. The authors admitted to having been inspired by Chargaff's discoveries, but they said little about the contributions of others such as Jerry Donohue—an expert on *hydrogen bonding* who had helped Watson and Crick realize that that was the type of bond holding the

The Structure of DNA

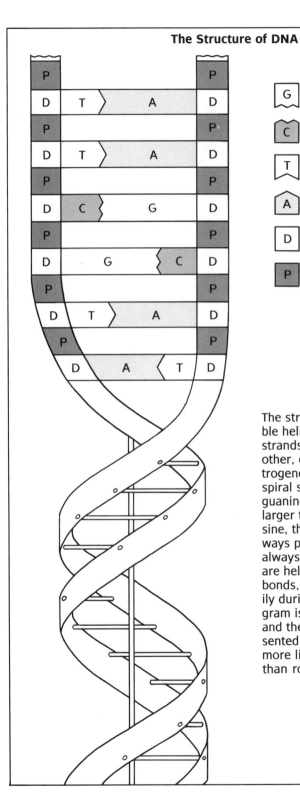

G	guanine
C	cytosine
T	thymine
A	adenine
D	deoxyribose
P	phosphate

The structure of DNA is a double helix: two phosphate-sugar strands wrapped around each other, connected by paired nitrogenous bases, much like a spiral staircase. Adenine and guanine, the purines, are larger than thymine and cytosine, the pyrimidines. A always pairs with T, and G always pairs with C. The bases are held together by hydrogen bonds, which come apart easily during replication. This diagram is not drawn to scale, and the base pairs, represented by rods, are actually more like flat "steps" than rods.

bases together—and John Griffith—a mathematician who calculated the way in which the bases paired up with each other (as had Chargaff).

The Watson-Crick model of the DNA molecule was a *double helix*, two helical strands wrapped around each other. The bases extend inward, not outward, like the steps in a circular stairway. An adenine in one strand is matched by a thymine in the other; a cytosine in one strand is matched by a guanine in the other. The dimensions of the four bases are such that the lengths of an adenine-thymine pair and a guanine-cytosine pair are identical. The phosphates form the backbone of the helix; the bases are joined by hydrogen bonds, a form of chemical linkage that can be broken fairly easily.

The Watson-Crick model provided an explanation of how a parent cell can provide identical copies of its genetic material to two offspring cells. Before cell division, the two strands of the DNA helix come apart. Enzymes in the cell then match each base of a strand with the appropriate base needed to form a double

This photo of the 1962 Nobel Prize winners shows, from left to right, Francis Crick, Maurice Wilkins, John Steinbeck, James Watson, Max Perutz, and John Kendrew. Crick, Watson, and Wilkins shared the prize in physiology or medicine for their work on the structure of DNA.

helix—an adenine nucleotide wherever there is a thymine, a cytosine nucleotide wherever there is a guanine, and so on. The end products are two complete DNA double helices, one for each offspring cell.

Although Watson and Crick were the first to put all the pieces together and publish a paper proposing a double helical structure for DNA, their research was aided by the information and ideas of many others. Maurice Wilkins shared their 1962 Nobel Prize in physiology or medicine, and it is highly probable that Rosalind Franklin would also have, had she lived that long. (The race to discover the structure of DNA has been brilliantly described in *The Double Helix*, a book by James Watson published in 1968, but it gives a somewhat one-sided version of the story. Anne Sayre's 1975 book *Rosalind Franklin and DNA* gives what might have been Franklin's point of view, had she lived. *In Search of the Double Helix*, John Gribbin's 1985 book, presents a more balanced, fascinating account of the story.)

In 1956, three years after Watson and Crick described the structure of DNA, Arthur Kornberg, of Washington University in St. Louis, proved their point. He first found an enzyme that catalyzed the formation of new DNA strands. He named it *DNA polymerase*. He then put all the ingredients needed to form DNA—nucleotides, enzymes, and so on—in a test tube with DNA from bacteria. New strands of DNA were created in the test tube, an achievement some awed observers described as no less than the creation of life. At the least, Kornberg showed that Watson and Crick's model was essentially correct. For this work, he (with Severo Ochoa) won the Nobel Prize in physiology or medicine in 1959.

•   •   •   •

CHAPTER 3

FROM GENE TO PROTEIN

T4 cells infected with HTLV-III, a retro-virus, magnified 111,000 times

The Watson-Crick model of DNA opened the door to other major advances. By the early 1950s, biologists knew that genes were composed of DNA and that they did their work by governing production of proteins. The next challenge was to map the road from gene to protein. The eventual map was the work of many scientists in many laboratories.

PROTEIN PRODUCTION

The site of protein production was found in the mid-1950s by two teams of American researchers, George E. Palade and Philip Siekevitz at the Rockefeller Institute and Paul C. Zamecnik and Mahlon Hoagland at Harvard. Using the electron microscope, Palade and Siekevitz discovered a new particle, the *ribosome*, in the cytoplasm of living cells. Ribosomes are the smallest intracellular units, and cells contain many thousands of them. Work by Palade, Siekevitz, and Zamecnik showed that ribosomes are rich in "the other" nucleic acid, RNA, and that they are primarily responsible for producing the cell's proteins.

RNA

To learn how a protein is assembled, Zamecnik and Hoagland began working with mixtures of amino acids and RNA. They found that before amino acid molecules were incorporated into a protein chain, they were linked to RNA molecules. In addition, they found that each of the 20 amino acids had its own specific RNA molecule that transferred it to the ribosomes. So there were two forms of RNA—the kind found in ribosomes, now called *ribosomal RNA*, and *transfer RNA*.

Then a third kind of RNA was discovered, by Elliot Volkin and Lazarus Astrachan at Oak Ridge National Laboratory in Tennessee, in 1956. It is called *messenger RNA* because it carries the genetic information for protein production from the nucleus to the ribosome. Messenger RNA, it was found, is made in strands that can be matched with specific segments of DNA in the nucleus—the genes. Just as one strand of DNA makes a complementary strand when the cell divides, a gene makes a complementary strand of RNA to start the process of protein production.

A complete map of the road from gene to protein was drawn in the early 1960s by two French scientists, François Jacob and Jacques-Lucien Monod, of the Pasteur Institute in Paris. One of their major contributions was to identify the element of control, demonstrating that small proteins called *repressors* govern gene activity. Each gene has its own repressor (made by an entirely different gene). The repressor molecule sits on the gene, blocking its activity. The process of protein formation begins when the repressor is pulled loose from the gene. The double strand of DNA encoding the gene unwinds. Enzymes then transcribe the genetic information in the gene to produce a strand of messenger RNA complementary to the segment of DNA (except that the RNA has a uracil base wherever DNA would have thymine).

When it is completed, the strand of messenger RNA moves out of the nucleus to a ribosome, where it starts the manufacture of a protein. Transfer RNA molecules, each with its amino acid attached, travel to the ribosome. Whenever the sequence of a transfer RNA molecule matches the sequence of the messenger RNA, that amino acid joins the protein chain. When the entire messenger RNA sequence has been read, the protein is released by the ribosome, which is then free to receive another messenger RNA molecule and start production of another protein. A *feedback process* ends protein production by putting the repressor back on the DNA segment encoding the gene. *Feedback* in this case means that when enough protein has been produced, a signal is sent that activates the gene for the repressor molecule. Jacob and Monod studied the gene for an enzyme that breaks down sugar molecules. The signal that acts on the repressor mol-

François Jacob, Jacques-Lucien Monod, and André-Michael Lwoff (left to right)—the three winners of the 1965 Nobel Prize in physiology or medicine, at the Pasteur Institute in Paris. Jacob and Monod discovered gene repressors.

ecule, they found, was the sugar molecules, which attach themselves to the repressor. When there is an ample supply of sugar molecules, they pull the repressor molecules off the gene. It goes into action, making enzymes that break down the sugar molecules. As the concentration of sugar falls, repressor molecules are freed and attach to the gene again, stopping its activity.

Sequencing

With the picture of gene activity clear, scientists moved on to the question, What is the genetic code that translates a sequence of nucleotides in DNA into the chain of amino acids that makes up a protein? Simple logic provided a major clue. There are 20 different amino acids, and there are 4 different nucleotides in DNA. One nucleotide obviously cannot code for one amino acid. Two-nucleotide sequences are not enough either because only 16 combinations are possible. Three-nucleotide sequences provide 64 combinations, which are more than enough.

Work by Francis Crick supported the three-nucleotide code theory. He worked with a *bacteriophage*, a *virus* that infects bacteria. Viruses are such simple things that they are regarded as not quite living organisms. A virus is an acellular parasite that consists of a few genes, in the form of either DNA or RNA, inside a protein coat. It reproduces by using its genes to take over the much more complicated systems of a living cell, making the cell into a virus-producing factory. The very simplicity of a virus makes it useful for some kinds of genetic experiments, such as those done by Crick.

Crick induced a series of mutations by adding or subtracting nucleotides from the genes of the virus. When he added or subtracted one nucleotide, the genes stopped working. The same thing happened when he added or subtracted two nucleotides. When he added or subtracted three nucleotides, the gene functioned, although the protein it produced was abnormal.

Crick also took a first step toward breaking the genetic code. He found certain three-nucleotide sequences that acted as punctuation marks. They did not code for amino acids but ended production of a protein by acting as periods at the end of a sentence. Work done by Linus Pauling in the late 1950s on *sickle-*

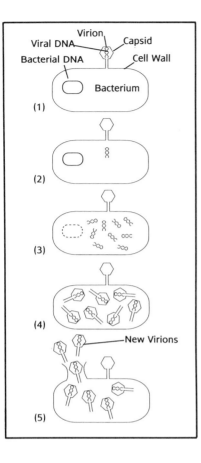

VIRAL REPRODUCTION

A virus must use a cell's reproductive mechanism to produce new virions. Shown at left, a type of virus called a bacteriophage attacks a bacterial cell. Other viruses attack the cells of organisms in much the same way. (1) A virion attaches to the cell wall of a bacterium and makes a hole in the cell wall. (2) Viral DNA enters the bacterium. (3) The viral DNA directs the cell to make replicas of the viral DNA. Bacterial DNA disappears. (4) New capsids are created. (5) The bacterium is destroyed. The cell wall releases new virions to repeat the process.

cell anemia also supported the idea of a three-nucleotide "word." The first three-nucleotide "word" for an amino acid in the genetic code was found in 1961 by Marshall W. Nirenberg and Johann Matthaei at the National Institutes of Health (NIH), drawing on discoveries of other scientists.

In the mid-1950s, at about the same time that Arthur Kornberg had discovered the enzyme that catalyzed production of DNA chains, Severo Ochoa and Marianne Grunberg-Manago at New York University had found an enzyme that did the same for RNA. Nirenberg used this *RNA polymerase* (so called because it catalyzes production of *polymers*, or long chains, of RNA) to make a synthetic RNA containing only uracil. When Nirenberg added these RNA strands (U-U-U-U-U-U, etc.) to a *cell-free system*, in this case, a mixture of ribosomes, enzymes, and amino acids, the result was a protein that contained only one amino acid, *phenylalanine*. Thus, UUU was the three-nucleotide RNA sequence that coded for phenylalanine. That sequence could be translated to DNA, which contains thymine instead of uracil. Thymine is complementary to adenine, so a UUU RNA sequence occurs wherever DNA has an AAA sequence.

MORE DISCOVERIES

The rest of the genetic code was worked out in several ways. One experiment used RNA chains consisting mostly of U with a relatively low proportion of A added. Three sequences that contained both U and A were isolated: UAU, UUA, AUU. The proteins that resulted contained mostly phenylalanine (from UUU) but also small amounts of three other amino acids, *leucine, isoleucine*, and *tyrosine*. Radioactively tagged strands of nucleic acids were used to determine which sequence produced which protein. Another method was to look at the amino acids attached to specific messenger RNA molecules. Messenger RNA uses a three-nucleotide sequence to bind an amino acid; the researchers painstakingly learned which sequence bound which amino acid. It did not take long before scientists believed they had unraveled the complete genetic code.

The picture seemed complete, so complete that it began to be called the "central dogma" of genetics: DNA in the nucleus makes RNA, which makes protein. The "central dogma" said genetic information moves only in one direction, outward from DNA. But a number of discoveries have shown that complexities in living cells resist the simplicity of this dogma.

Organelles and Plasmids

It was discovered that not all the DNA in a cell is in the nucleus. Some of it is in the *mitochondria*, the small bodies that serve as the powerhouses of the cell. Mitochondria are a type of *organelle* (a membrane-bound structure within a cell). They are the site of the chemical reactions that extract energy from *fats* (substances containing one or more fatty acid) and carbohydrates. Mitochondrial DNA is unusual because it is inherited only from the mother. An egg is big enough to contain mitochondria, whereas a sperm is not, having just enough room for the male chromosome. It is generally assumed that mitochondria once were free-living organisms that over long periods of time became incorporated in larger cells. Their genes perform essential functions in the cell. Plant cells have analogous bodies called *chloroplasts*, which provide plant energy through the conversion of sunlight. These organelles, too, have their own DNA and are believed to have originated as free-living organisms.

A cell with a nucleus defined by a cell membrane is a *eukaryote*. All the cells in the human body (and in any multicellular organism) are eukaryotic. A cell without a nucleus is a *prokaryote*. Bacteria are prokaryotic. Their chromosomes, which are loop shaped, float freely in the cytoplasm. Bacteria also contain other, smaller loops of DNA called *plasmids*. A plasmid is more a resident of a bacterium than it is a part of it. The relationship is *symbiotic*, meaning that each partner benefits from the other. The plasmid gets security, the bacteria gets some additional genes for traits such as resistance to antibiotics. One reason doctors are told to limit use of antibiotics is that plasmid genes can mutate to cause resistance to the drugs. Bacterial plasmids transfer easily among bacteria cells, so resistance can spread fast.

A plasmid seems simple enough, just some mildly useful extra baggage for bacteria, but it has become enormously useful to humankind. A plasmid, in fact, is a foundation on which the major new industry of *genetic engineering* has been built.

Beyond the "Central Dogma"

New discoveries have continued to extend scientists' knowledge of genetics. One discovery was that genetic information does not always flow from DNA to RNA. Some viruses have RNA as their genetic material. They make an enzyme called *reverse transcriptase*, which translates RNA into DNA. They are called *retroviruses*. The first virus to be identified as a cause of cancer in humans was a retrovirus, *HTLV-1* (human T-cell leukemia virus). Another retrovirus, *HIV* (human immunodeficiency virus) is even better known. It causes *AIDS* (acquired immune deficiency syndrome)—a contagious defect of the immune system, spread by contaminated blood, sexual contact, or nutritive fluids passed from a mother to a fetus, that leaves people vulnerable to certain specific diseases and infections, which then almost always prove fatal. Mainly because of AIDS, retroviruses began to be studied very intensively during the 1980s and early 1990s.

New discoveries have often brought with them new complications. One puzzle is that human genes contain large segments that appear to be meaningless. When the gene is expressed (meaning that it goes into action to produce protein), the meaningless segments dutifully turn into messenger RNA, but these segments are cut out before the messenger RNA leaves the nucleus. The meaningless segments of a gene are called *introns*. The sections carrying information are called *exons*. No one knows why nature has included so much apparently meaningless information in human genes.

In 1951, Barbara McClintock, a researcher at Cold Spring Harbor Laboratory on Long Island, New York, discovered that genes do not always remain stationary. Working with corn plants, McClintock found what scientists call *transposable elements*, or transpos, and journalists like to call "jumping genes," which move from place to place on a chromosome or even from one chromosome to another. McClintock worked with the genes for the color of the kernels of corn, so she could see when a gene had jumped by a change in the pigmentation in an ear of corn.

It appears that jumping genes can synthesize enzymes that cut them free from their location on the chromosome. Once free, they can move to another chromosomal location or can even be picked up by a retrovirus and carried to another cell or organism. Transpos are believed to play an important role in evolution by causing major mutations—for example, by producing chromosome breaks.

A kind of gene shuffling that occurs in cells of the *immune system* (the body's natural system of defense) makes it possible for the body to defend itself against a myriad of foreign invaders such as viruses and bacteria. A front line of defense is the production of *antibodies*, proteins that recognize foreign molecules called *antigens*. There are almost an endless number of antigens. The puzzle was how the body could make an antibody for every antigen. The answer lay in the genes of *B cells*, white blood cells that produce antigens.

The antibody genes of a B cell do not consist of continuous segments of DNA. Instead, they are assembled from hundreds of bits and pieces of DNA that are scattered on different chromosomes. When an individual B cell matures, it rearranges these segments, cutting some out and splicing others together until it creates a gene for a unique antibody. All the descendants of that B cell will carry this unique gene. Mutations take place in future generations, allowing the production of antibodies that can react to slightly different antigens. When an appropriate antigen appears, the B cells carrying the gene for the corresponding antibody multiply rapidly, producing antibodies that overwhelm the invader. Thus, a limited number of genes can produce an unlimited variety of antibodies.

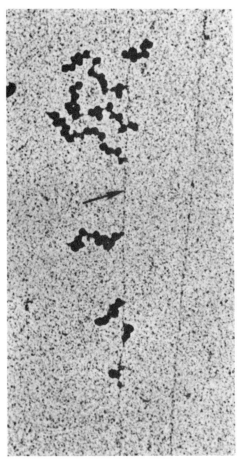

A gene is expressed when it produces a protein. This 1970 photo is the first ever taken of protein synthesis. Taken through an electron microscope, it shows chromosomes (indicated by the arrow), magnified 110,000 times, as they direct the formation of protein molecules on the beadlike strings of granules (polyribosomes) that extend from them.

One more important fact is that there is great variation in the DNA of members of the same species, including humans. The basic design is the same, but the sequence of bases in a gene (and so of the amino acids in a protein) tends to vary from individual to individual. This common, normal variation is called *DNA polymorphism*. As Chapters 7 and 9 will show, it is becoming increasingly important in medical genetics and basic research.

The complexity of the genetic system is awesome. As stated above, there are genes that control other genes, genes that jump, genes that are shuffled. Yet scientific understanding of genetics is such that it is now possible to manipulate the system to serve many human ends through genetic engineering, the subject of the next chapter.

●　　　●　　　●　　　●

CHAPTER 4

GENETIC ENGINEERING

H. Gobind Khorana (right) and colleague

In 1973, after years of work, H. Gobind Khorana and his colleagues at the Massachusetts Institute of Technology (MIT) made the first synthetic gene. They laboriously linked nucleotide after nucleotide until they had the exact DNA sequence that would create the transfer RNA for the amino acid tyrosine. It was a momentous achievement but an incomplete one. Khorana's synthetic gene could not be expressed to make the strand of RNA because the necessary control sequences were not there.

As already described, a gene is a segment of DNA that codes for a protein. As Khorana's effort showed, this definition was incomplete. In a living organism, that segment of DNA requires helpers and controlling mechanisms. It needs signals to turn it off and on and enzymes to transcribe it. It is possible to make a gene work in a cell-free system by supplying all the proper helpers and controls, but that achievement is not terribly productive. A much more powerful technique is to use the existing mechanisms of a living cell. That enterprise is genetic engineering. It is one of the most impressive—to some people one of the most frightening—achievements of 20th-century science; one that will affect all people.

RECOMBINANT DNA

The story of genetic engineering is a story of many scientific discoveries coming together. One of these occurred in 1971, when two American microbiologists, Daniel Nathans and Hamilton O. Smith, found that cells contain enzymes that can recognize a specific sequence of nucleotides in a strand of DNA and that can cut the strand at that point. There are dozens, perhaps hundreds, of these *restriction enzymes*. It is believed that they help defend cells against viruses by attacking viral DNA. Their discovery gave biologists a way to snip out segments of DNA for detailed study.

Paul Berg, a biochemist at Stanford University, picked up the discovery that same year and took one of the first important steps toward genetic engineering. Berg was studying the control of gene expression—how genes are turned on and off. He decided to extract DNA from a virus and insert it into bacterial cells. Berg used restriction enzymes to cleave the DNA of a virus named *SV40*. To meet the next challenge, insertion of the segment of DNA into bacteria, Berg developed an ingenious method. He first added short "tails" of single-stranded DNA to each end of the segment. These tails were "sticky"; they would attach themselves to complementary single strands of DNA.

Then Berg took DNA from a bacteriophage, cleaved it with restriction enzymes, and attached sticky tails of DNA to those segments. He joined the SV40 DNA and bacteriophage DNA, making a single molecule of *recombinant DNA*. He wrapped this hybrid gene in the protein coat of the bacteriophage. The result was a virus that would infect bacteria, carrying a hybrid gene with it. Berg stopped there (for reasons that will be explained shortly), but others were undertaking equally momentous steps.

The two major players were Stanley Cohen and Herbert Boyer. Cohen was working at Stanford University with plasmids, those loops of DNA found in bacteria. Trying to isolate the gene for antibiotic resistance from the plasmids, Cohen broke them apart by whirling them in a *centrifuge* (a machine that rapidly spins a sample, separating various components) and studied the resulting fragments.

It was at a scientific meeting in Hawaii that Cohen met Boyer, an expert on restriction enzymes at the University of California at San Francisco. The two sat down to a now-famous late dinner in a Waikiki delicatessen and began comparing notes. Boyer told Cohen how restriction enzymes could cut DNA at specified points. He described one restriction enzyme, called *EcoRI*, that even produced the sticky ends Berg was working so hard to make. By the time the meal was through, Boyer and Cohen were well on the way toward a method of inserting new genetic information into bacteria.

Boyer would supply the restriction enzymes, Cohen the plasmids. Back in California, Cohen found a plasmid with just one site that would be cut by EcoRI. Boyer's restriction enzyme sliced it open. Boyer and Cohen inserted genes from *Staphylococcus* (an infection-causing bacterium) and from a toad cell and then put the plasma into *Escherichia coli* (also called *E. coli*), a harmless sort of bacterium that inhabits the human gut. Tests showed the genes inserted into the bacteria expressed themselves, producing proteins. The first genetically engineered organisms had been created.

It did not take long for many biologists to realize that recombinant DNA technology had enormous scientific and commercial possibilities—and also areas of potential danger. Scientifically, recombinant DNA offered a way to isolate and study genes. A biologist could slice a segment of DNA from a chromosome, insert it into a bacterium, and find out whether the bacterium would start making an unusual protein. If it did, the gene for that protein was in the inserted segment of DNA. The biologist could then study the gene and its control mechanisms in detail.

Commercially, recombinant DNA offered a method of mass-producing specific proteins. Isolate the gene for a protein, insert it in bacteria, grow huge vats of the bacteria, and the result is a biological protein factory. Some candidates for recombinant DNA production presented themselves immediately—*insulin* (a hormone that metabolizes sugar; used to treat diabetes), which was then obtained entirely from animal pancreases and *human growth hormone* (a hormone that stimulates growth; used to treat dwarfism), tiny amounts of which were painstakingly extracted from human pituitary glands after death.

Biohazards

The first alarm about the possible danger of recombinant DNA technology was raised by Robert Pollack, a microbiologist at Cold Spring Harbor Laboratory on Long Island. He heard about Berg's

Midgets, people suffering from a form of dwarfism, can be treated with human growth hormone (HGH). HGH was once available only through extraction from the human pituitary gland after the death of a donor. Now, genetically engineered bacteria can produce the hormone.

SV40 experiment from a visiting scientist and pointed out one risk. The SV40 virus is known to cause tumors in some animals, although it has not been shown to be harmful to humans. Pollack asked what might happen if an altered bacterium with SV40 genes escaped from the laboratory dish and infected someone. Might it cause cancer? Might its genes combine with bacteria in the body to produce a virulent hybrid? Might it spread outside the laboratory to cause a plague?

The questions raised by Pollack eventually resulted in an open letter signed by 78 scientists that appeared in *Science* in September 1973. It said recombinant DNA work "may prove hazardous to laboratory workers and to the public" and asked for a committee to set guidelines. In 1974, Berg and other scientists wrote another letter that went even further, proposing a voluntary moratorium on further experimentation with genetic engineering techniques "until the potential hazards of such recombinant DNA molecules have been better evaluated or more adequate methods are developed for preventing their spread." This letter was published simultaneously in three British and American science journals.

It was a unique event in science. Never before had scientists proposed a self-enforcing halt in experiments because of potential danger. The closest parallel occurred in the years of World War II, when nuclear physicists realized that an atomic bomb was possible and that Adolf Hitler might make one. Even then, the physicists did not propose to stop their experiments, only to keep them secret.

The upshot of the letter was an international meeting held in 1975 at Asilomar, California, where the world's leading molecular biologists thrashed out the issue. They produced a set of proposed safety procedures that centered on two methods of reducing danger. One was the use of laboratory containment systems (special protective equipment and procedures that prevent experimental materials from escaping into the environment) for potentially dangerous experiments. The second was development of deliberately weakened bacteria that could not live outside a laboratory dish.

Both methods were adopted. Biotechnology laboratories are now classified from P1 to P4, depending on the degree of confinement. The most dangerous experiments are reserved for P4 laboratories, in which workers wear special clothes and use elaborate containment devices. In addition, most experimenters began using a weakened strain of *E. coli* that could not survive outside a laboratory dish. Nonetheless, the debate about the risks of recombinant DNA technology goes on.

Commercial Uses

Recombinant DNA technology continues. One of the crucial developments was the use of a region of a gene called a *promoter* to increase its expression. The techniques Cohen and Boyer developed proved inadequate for commercial use because the yield of the desired protein was too small. Researchers turned to the control mechanism that Jacob and Monod had described. The actual repressor had been isolated by Walter Gilbert, Benno Mueller-Hill, and Mark Ptashne at Harvard University. They called it the *lac gene* because it controlled the gene for the enzyme that breaks down *lactose* (a simple sugar). By 1976, the Harvard group and scientists at the University of California were linking the lac promoter with a DNA segment designed to insert the desired gene, whose expression would be started by the promoter.

Another advance was the use of a different enzyme to join DNA molecules. Making sticky ends was laborious work. A better way emerged when Vittorio Sgaramella, a scientist in Khorana's MIT laboratory, discovered *DNA ligase*, an enzyme that joins DNA strands without sticky ends.

Recombinant DNA technology has advanced in many such steps. Many of the techniques now used were pioneered in a race to produce human insulin through genetic engineering. The race was between Harvard scientist Walter Gilbert and his colleagues, and the eventual winner, a West Coast group connected with Genentech, Inc., a biotechnology company founded by Boyer, and assisted by Arthur D. Riggs at the City of Hope National Medical Center.

The next protein genetic engineering was to produce commercially was human growth hormone, which treats children who would otherwise be abnormally short because their *pituitary glands* (endocrine glands) do not produce growth hormone. Another recombinant DNA product in wide medical use is *tissue plasminogen activator* (TPA), which dissolves blood clots. It is infused into the bloodstream soon after a heart attack to dissolve clots blocking the coronary arteries, thus reducing damage to the heart muscle and improving the chance of survival. More recombinant DNA products appear every year.

Transgenic Animals

A very new frontier is the modification of living animals by insertion of genes. The creation of *transgenic* animals is a more difficult challenge than engineering bacteria because the gene must not only be inserted in such a way that it is under the appropriate genetic controls, expressing itself in the proper tissue at the proper time, but also must be fitted into the proper cells.

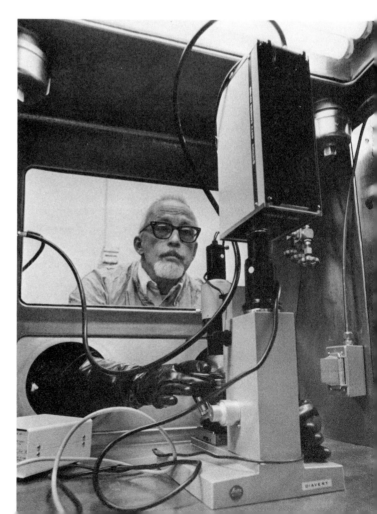

A remote-control electronic microscope for use in recombinant DNA research is set up in a containment chamber. Confined work areas such as this one help prevent the release of genetically altered organisms into the environment.

Transgenic animals are made by inserting a gene into fertilized eggs or very early embryos. Several methods are available. The most common one is to inject multiple copies of a gene into each fertilized egg, which is then implanted in a surrogate mother animal. A second method is to put the gene into a specially altered retrovirus. The retrovirus inserts the gene by infecting cells of an early embryo. A third method is to extract cells from an early embryo, transfer the gene through injection or retrovirus infection, and place the cells in another embryo. The animal grows up to be a chimera, with some cells carrying genes from the animal that provided the egg and the animal that fertilized the egg and some from the animal whose genes were inserted. One such animal, produced in England, is a "geep," half goat and half sheep.

None of these techniques works as efficiently as one may desire. Biologists do not know how an injected gene is incorporated in the chromosomes of an animal cell and cannot direct it to the proper location. The location of a gene is critical to the cell's survival and the gene's performance. Only about 2% of fertilized eggs survive gene injection, for example. But a single success can lead to a new line of animals with altered genetic characteristics.

One of the early successes, made in 1983 by Ralph Brinster of the University of Pennsylvania and Richard Palmiter of the University of Washington, was the insertion of the growth hormone gene into mice, which then grew to be twice the size of their litter mates. The same scientists also inserted the growth hormone gene into pigs, but in this case, for unknown reasons, none of the pigs grew bigger.

In Britain, John Clark of the Agricultural and Food Council has introduced genes for important human proteins into the mammary glands of animals. The animal then becomes a protein factory, producing the protein in its milk. If the yield of protein can be increased to commercial levels, such altered animals could displace genetically engineered bacteria because it is easier to tend small herds of animals than vast tanks of bacteria. A project of several companies in the United States is the insertion into dairy cattle of the gene for bovine somatotropin, a hormone that increases an animal's milk production by up to 30%.

In the laboratory, transgenic mice have become commonplace.

In 1988, Harvard University patented the transgenic mouse shown here with genetics professor Philip Leder. This was the first time a patent had been issued for an animal.

For research purposes, many laboratories insert genes for specific medical conditions into mice. Transgenic mice have been created for research in cancer, heart disease, and dozens of other medical conditions.

In 1988, the first U.S. patent for a living animal was awarded to Harvard University for a transgenic mouse carrying an *activated oncogene sequence* that made it more susceptible to cancer-causing substances. (An oncogene is a gene that is involved in the process by which a cell is transformed from normal to malignant.)

These developments—the creation and patenting of transgenic animals—are controversial. Critics have objected to human interference with the genetic substance of animals and plants on ethical grounds. They add that transgenic animal technology will benefit large agribusiness corporations at the expense of small farmers, who will not be able to pay the prices genetic engineers demand. Proponents say humans have always altered animals through breeding for their own purposes and that genetic technology is simply a more effective way to reach an old goal. They point to anticipated benefits: improved productivity, better understanding of disease, even a way to cure some human genetic diseases.

This last proposal, human gene therapy, has aroused the greatest controversy of all. Chapter 7 discusses this further. But first, one should explore some basic scientific applications of the new genetics.

•   •   •   •

CHAPTER 5

SCIENCE AND GENES

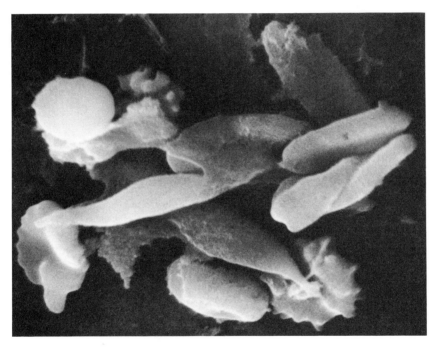

Human sickle cells magnified 8,000 times

As is often the case in science, discoveries build on discoveries, and researchers who set out to investigate one thing often learn about others. Chapter 3 mentioned that Linus Pauling's work on sickle-cell anemia supported the theory of the three–nitrogenous base "word" being developed in the 1950s. He had not begun by studying the problem of how many bases made up a "word." He had begun by studying sickle-cell anemia.

SICKLE-CELL ANEMIA

Linus Pauling first became interested in sickle-cell anemia after World War II, in the late 1940s, while he was on a committee formed to advise the U.S. government on what areas of medical research to fund. There is a high incidence of sickle-cell anemia in the black population of central Africa and other tropical regions, where it is often fatal. Those with sickle-cell anemia suffer from mild to severe anemia and can experience sickle-cell attacks, leading to organ damage, severe infection, or death.

Sickle-cell anemia is a recessive hereditary disease named for the unusual shape of red blood cells found in its victims. Instead

Linus Pauling in 1985. Pauling discovered that the defective element in sickle-cell anemia was hemoglobin; when it gives up O_2, the red blood cell collapses, or sickles.

of the normal disklike shape, the cells become sickle shaped when they pass from the *arteries* (blood vessels that carry blood away from the heart) into the *veins* (blood vessels that carry blood back to the heart). Normally, the *hemoglobin* (a protein that serves as a pigment and carries oxygen and carbon dioxide in the blood) in each red blood cell attaches to an oxygen molecule when the blood passes through the lungs. The red blood cell then carries this oxygen to areas of the body in need of it, at which point it releases the oxygen and picks up a molecule of *carbon dioxide* (a cellular waste product) and brings it back to the lungs to be exhaled.

Pauling's investigations showed that the source of the problem in sickle-cell anemia was in hemoglobin. Hemoglobin from sickle-cell patients looks and acts normal while it carries oxygen in the arteries. When the hemoglobin gives up its oxygen, at the time when the red blood cell enters the veins for the return trip to the heart, the hemoglobin molecule can no longer maintain its normal shape and collapses. The cell collapses with it.

In the mid-1950s, the British scientist Vernon Ingram took Pauling's finding one step further. The cause of the collapse, Ingram found, was a change in 1 amino acid of the almost 600 that make up the hemoglobin molecule. At one point in the abnormal protein, a *valine* replaces the amino acid *glutamic acid*. That alters the chemical properties of the molecule profoundly enough to cause the collapse. It was later found that the three-nucleotide code in DNA for glutamic acid is either CTT or CTC. The code for valine can be CAT, CAC, or two other combinations. (Amino acids are often coded by more than one three-nucleotide sequence.) So the substitution of an A for a T, changing CTT to CAT, or the substitution of an A for a T, changing CTC to CAC, can change the amino acid created. A single change in the nucleotide chain—a *point mutation*, it is called—is enough to cause the immense problem of sickle-cell anemia.

If such a mutation is so damaging, one would think that the gene for it would eventually disappear because people who carry it are more likely to die young without passing on the mutation to offspring. The sickle-cell anemia gene persists because it is not strictly harmful. A *single* mutated gene protects the carrier from *malaria* (a sometimes fatal protozoal disease carried by mosquitoes) that is common in parts of Africa. (*Two* mutated genes, however, express themselves as sickle-cell anemia.) The advantage one gene gives more than balances, in terms of overall survival, the damage done to people who have the bad luck to inherit two mutated genes. As many as 25% of Africans in malaria-prone areas carry the sickle-cell gene.

POINT MUTATIONS

Chapter 6 discusses genetic diseases at length. This chapter will concentrate on the scientific aspects of point mutations. Their existence has resulted in some valuable scientific advances and some major controversies, both in the area of evolution.

A major fact about point mutations is that they are very common. Many enzymes have been found to have alternative versions that differ by one or more amino acids, which means that there are different versions of the genes for those proteins. Different versions of the same gene are called *alleles*. This can mean an allele for brown eyes and one for blue eyes, or it can mean an allele for a certain amino acid sequence for a protein and one for a variation of the amino acid sequence for the same protein. In many cases, a mutation in DNA that results in the substitution of one amino acid for another does not affect the function of an enzyme. (If the mutation does prevent the enzyme from functioning properly, it is likely to kill the individual carrying the flawed enzyme before that individual reproduces and thus destroy the mutated gene.) But these mutations can be used to determine how one individual is related to another or how one species is related to another.

Start with individuals in the same species—the human species, for example. All humans carry the same basic set of enzymes and genes for those enzymes. But they do not all carry the same alleles for all those genes. Indeed, aside from identical twins (who arise from the same fertilized egg), it is highly probable that no two people on earth are alike genetically. Someone who looked methodically at all of an individual's genes would find some of them different from those of that person's brother or sister. The differences would be greater for his or her cousins and still greater for more distant relatives.

With the exception of identical twins, no two people have exactly the same genetic information. Differences are minimal for fraternal twins and become greater as the relation between the individuals becomes more distant.

Scientists can—and do—look systematically at the genetic differences of individuals from different families and ethnic groups. Such studies can produce an evolutionary tree showing how closely one ethnic group is related to another. It is even possible to work out indicators of how humans spread from their original source, believed to be Africa, all over the world.

This sort of study is possible because mutations happen all the time, for a variety of reasons: A DNA strand is copied imperfectly, natural radiation strikes a cell, a naturally occurring chemical affects DNA, and so on. Some point mutations garble the genetic message so badly that the cell cannot survive. Some, like the sickle-cell mutation, cause lesser kinds of damage. A few are favorable. And many are neutral: They cause one amino acid to be substituted for another in a protein, but the activity of the protein is not affected one way or the other. About 150 mutant forms of hemoglobin have been found in human beings, for example. A few are harmful. Most have no effect at all.

MOLECULAR EVOLUTION

Most animal species come outfitted with a basic set of genes that have survived for billions of years. Any creature, from a one-celled yeast to a human, must carry out essential activities, such as obtaining energy from food. They use a basic set of enzymes for such activities. One such enzyme is *cytochrome c*, which is essential for energy production. Cytochrome c has been extracted from many species, and its amino acid sequence has been worked out. In the 1960s, Walter Fitch and Emanuel Margoliash of Northwestern University in Evanston, Illinois, began to study the differences in the amino acid sequences of cytochrome c molecules from a number of species. They found small differences between closely related species, larger differences between distantly related sequences. Working backward from those differences, they were able to build an evolution tree, showing the order in which one species diverged from another.

A number of scientists are now working in this field of *molecular evolution*. At Yale University in 1986, for example, Charles Sibley and his co-workers built a complete evolutionary tree of birds by comparing differences in a number of enzymes. The work that has received the most attention is on human evolution. Two of the major figures in this field, Vincent Sarich and Allan Wilson of the University of California at Berkeley, did much of their work as early as 1965.

They compared the molecular sequences of substances such as *albumin*, a blood protein, from primates, the group that includes monkeys, apes, and humans. The conclusions that aroused the greatest controversy were that the closest relative of the human species is the chimpanzee, with the gorilla next closest, and that humans, chimpanzees, and gorillas shared a common ancestor no more than 5 million years ago.

A controversy continues about these conclusions and others in the field of molecular evolution because the subject has uncertainties. One is whether mutations occur at a steady rate. Some scientists feel they do; others feel that mutations tend to come in bursts, occurring most rapidly when one species diverges from another. The molecules themselves are imperfect guides to the rate of mutation: They show whether mutations have occurred but not when they did. Other controversies center on how the molecular evidence is used to build evolutionary trees. Often, the same pattern can be assembled in different ways.

Neutral Mutations

Another scientific controversy concerns the evolutionary meaning of *neutral mutations*, those that neither help nor harm an individual. The modern version of the Darwinian theory of evolution says that neutral mutations have only a minor effect. According to the theory, the important mutations are those that either improve or impair function. Genes that improve function increase the probability that an individual will live to have viable offspring; genes that impair function decrease that probability. As mentioned, the Darwinian theory is that natural selection gradually weeds out detrimental mutations and leads to the spread of beneficial mutations, resulting in changes that eventually produce new species.

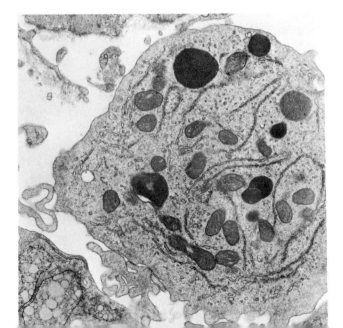

This electron micrograph of a plasma cell shows mitochondria, the smaller black organelles. Because mitochondrial DNA is passed on solely by the mother, its mutations can be used to trace families more easily than can those of nuclear DNA.

The large number of neutral mutations has led to a different theory, one of whose leading proponents is Motoo Kimura, a Japanese population geneticist. Kimura's theory is that the steady accumulation of neutral mutations, not natural selection, is the driving force in evolution. It says that new species arise not because natural selection acts on favorable and unfavorable mutations but because of a kind of *genetic drift* (the chance incorporation of a mutant gene into the gene pool of a small population) caused by the pileup of neutral mutations. Kimura's neutral gene theory of evolution is decidedly a minority view at this time.

The study of mitochondrial DNA has also produced some controversial results—notably the contention that all humans descended from a small group of women, perhaps only 1 woman, who lived in Africa 200,000 years ago. Mitochondria are the structures in the cell where energy is obtained from food. As mentioned, they have their own DNA, and the theory is that mitochondria once were independent organisms that were absorbed into cells. A single mitochondrion has 36 genes made up of 16,000 nucleotides. Mitochondrial genes mutate about 10 times faster than do genes in the cell nucleus. And mitochondrial genes are passed on only by the mother because eggs have mitochondria but sperm do not. Thus, by analyzing mutations in human mitochondrial DNA, it is possible to construct a family tree of the human race.

Allan Wilson, of the University of California at Berkeley, is one of several scientists who have constructed such family trees, comparing nucleotide sequences from humans all over the world. By assuming that neutral mutations in mitochondrial DNA accumulate at a steady rate, Wilson builds a family tree with two primary branches. One leads to people of African background, the other to most other humans. Wilson's calculations lead to the conclusion that there was a primeval "Eve" who passed her mitochondrial DNA on to all the humans alive today and that she lived in Africa anywhere from 140,000 to 290,000 years ago, with 200,000 years the best estimate. Such conclusions are controversial but illustrate the power of modern genetic techniques.

•　　　•　　　•　　　•

GENETIC DISEASES

Detail from El Niño de Vallecas *(1637) by Diego Velázquez shows a dwarf with Down's syndrome*

Genetic diseases are surprisingly common. Using the broadest definition, 1 of every 10 Americans suffers a genetic disorder. Some of these are caused by disorders of the chromosomes. These include *Down's syndrome* and some kinds of cancer. Other diseases are caused by defects in single genes. These include *Tay-Sachs disease, Huntington's chorea* (also known as Huntington's disease), *cystic fibrosis,* and *muscular dystrophy.* Certain genetic diseases are acquired by inheriting two recessive genes, as in sickle-cell anemia, or by a male inheriting an X chromosome carrying a defective gene. Many genetic disorders result from an interaction between genes and environmental factors. Diseases in this category include *diabetes, rheumatoid arthritis, schizophrenia*, and some forms of heart disease.

Human knowledge of genetic diseases is relatively new, dating back not further than the 1950s. The exception to that statement is an inspired discovery made at the turn of the century by Sir Archibald Garrod, a British physician and biochemist. In 1902, he identified a condition called alkaptonuria, in which the urine turns black, as a genetic condition inherited by Mendelian rules. Garrod even stated correctly that *alkaptonuria* was caused by the malfunction of a specific enzyme. It took a half century for medicine and science to catch up with Garrod's insight.

The delay is understandable. As shown, the nature and function of genes did not become clear until the 1950s. And it was only in 1956 that scientists got a correct count for the number of chromosomes in a human cell. They had thought there were 48; in fact there are 46, 2 matched sets of 23 each.

Genetic diseases and related research have become increasingly important in the past decades. One reason is that medicine has conquered many of the old killers, mainly infectious diseases. Another is the rapid growth of knowledge about genetics, which makes it possible to identify, diagnose, and, in some cases, treat genetic conditions. Researchers have identified more than 4,000 conditions caused by defective genes, and the number grows continually. Scientists have described hundreds of chromosomal disorders.

Genetic diseases often tend to run in ethnic groups. As seen, sickle-cell anemia occurs primarily in people of African descent. Tay-Sachs disease occurs mostly in Jews of eastern European origin. But it is vital to understand that no one is immune to genetic disease. It is estimated that each person carries at least 6 and perhaps as many as 20 potentially fatal recessive genes, which are expressed only if 2 people who carry the same gene have children. In addition, genetic diseases are not always inherited. Mutations or chromosomal abnormalities can occur at any time. People afflicted by genetic disease are no more flawed than anyone else. They have just had worse luck.

CHROMOSOME MUTATIONS

The imperfection of nature is largely responsible for mutations. Textbooks tend to describe the division of chromosomes in meiosis and mitosis as a flawless process. In fact, it often goes wrong. Chromosome damage can take several forms:

- *Deletion*—in which a section of a chromosome breaks off and is not incorporated into the new chromosome.

- *Duplication*—in which a section of a chromosome breaks away and attaches to the other chromosome in the pair.

- *Inversion*—in which a section of a chromosome is in reverse order in the new chromosome.

- *Translocation*—in which a section of a chromosome breaks away and attaches to a chromosome not part of the pair.

- *Crossing-over*—in which segments are exchanged by two paired chromosomes.

- *Nondisjunction*—in which the two chromosomes of a pair fail to separate during meiosis, resulting in a "pair" with an extra chromosome and a "pair" with only one chromosome.

The first chromosomal disease to be identified was Down's syndrome, a major cause of mental retardation. Down's syndrome was first described in 1866 by John Down, a British doctor. In 1959, 3 French geneticists, Jerome Lejeune, Marthe Gautier, and Raymond Turpin, studied cells from patients with the condition and found that each had 47 chromosomes, not the normal 46. The presence of an extra chromosome 21 (called *trisomy 21*) caused the disease. (Each human chromosome can be identified by its shape and other characteristics, and so all have been numbered.) The extra chromosome was the result of nondisjunction.

Chromosome Mutations

Normal mitosis produces two identical, diploid daughter cells, or cells that contain the same number of pairs as the parent cell.

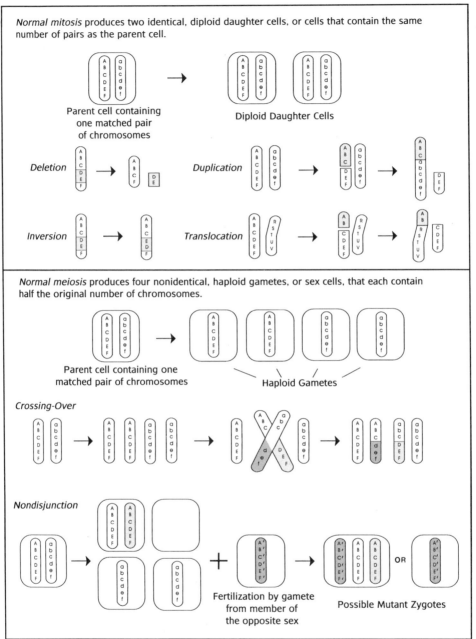

Parent cell containing one matched pair of chromosomes

Diploid Daughter Cells

Deletion

Duplication

Inversion

Translocation

Normal meiosis produces four nonidentical, haploid gametes, or sex cells, that each contain half the original number of chromosomes.

Parent cell containing one matched pair of chromosomes

Haploid Gametes

Crossing-Over

Nondisjunction

Fertilization by gamete from member of the opposite sex

Possible Mutant Zygotes

Letters signify specific segments of chromosome containing specific genes. Uppercase and lowercase letters indicate versions of the same genes on each of two chromosomes in a pair. Letters and the same letter with a prime indicate versions of the same genes on chromosomes from different gametes.

Several other genetic conditions in which there are an abnormal number of chromosomes due to nondisjunction have been described. One is *Klinefelter's syndrome*, which occurs only in boys and was described in the 1930s by an American doctor, Harry F. Klinefelter. Boys with Klinefelter's syndrome are sterile and are mentally retarded. A comparable condition in girls is *Turner's syndrome* (discovered by American physician Henry H. Turner), which also causes sterility and mental retardation. Both are disorders of the sex chromosomes. Klinefelter's syndrome patients have an extra X chromosome: Instead of being XY, they are XXY. Turner's syndrome patients have only one, not two, X chromosomes.

Turner's syndrome poses a question. How can individuals survive with a missing chromosome, an abnormality that usually is fatal? The answer is that the X chromosomes in females are unusual. One of them is always turned off. The first evidence for this finding came in 1949, when Murray L. Barr and E. G. Bertram of the University of Western Ontario found a dark object in nerve cells from female cats, but not in males. Proof that the *Barr body* is an inactivated X chromosome came in the 1950s from Mary Lyon, a British researcher. Studying mice that carried mutations for coat colors, she found the females had coats with patches of all the possible colors. The gene for coat color is on the X chromosome, and one of the X chromosomes in each cell is turned off early in life, Lyon showed. Apparently, pure chance determines whether the X from the father or the X from the mother is turned off. All females thus are genetic mosaics, made up of cells that differ slightly because of the inactivated X chromosome.

As in the case of extra or missing chromosomes, fragmentation of chromosomes can also cause disease. The first such fragment to be discovered was the *Philadelphia chromosome*, a broken-off section of chromosome 9 translocated to chromosome 22. It was found in cells from a leukemia patient in that city in 1959. Many more translocations associated with cancer have since been identified. The discovery of oncogenes has helped clarify why translocations cause cancer. Oncogenes are genes that play the crucial role in the transformation of a cell from normal to malignant. Oncogenes have been found at the site of cancer-associated translocations. The breaking of the chromosome starts the malignant activity of the oncogene.

GENE DEFECTS

Mutation or malfunction of individual genes can also cause disease. There are two basic kinds of genes: recessive and dominant. Two abnormal recessive genes are necessary to cause some diseases—as is the case in sickle-cell anemia. A single abnormal dominant gene can cause other diseases.

Possibly the best-known dominant genetic disorder is Huntington's chorea, which afflicted the folk singer Woody Guthrie. Someone who carries the Huntington's chorea gene is healthy for the first few decades of life, then begins a slow, unstoppable deterioration of the nervous system that eventually is fatal. The child of a parent with Huntington's chorea has a 50% chance of inheriting the fatal gene. Because the effects of the disease usually do not appear until late in the reproductive years, the gene can be passed on for many generations. In the 1980s, it became possible to tell some young people in Huntington's chorea families whether they carried the gene, using a technique to be discussed later. This technique can present young people from these families with a dilemma. Do they really want to know whether they carry the Huntington's chorea gene and, thus, will develop the disease themselves?

Many people these days do know whether they carry a gene for a recessive genetic disease. Several thousand of these diseases have been described and cataloged. Most are limited to a small number of people, many to a single family. Some of the more common conditions (cystic fibrosis, sickle-cell anemia, Tay-Sachs disease) have been mentioned. There are many more, including *phenylketonuria* (PKU); branched-chain ketonuria, or *maple sugar urine disease* (MSUD); *galactosemia*; and *hypothyroidism*.

To speak of a "common" recessive genetic illness is to use a relative term. Even common genetic diseases are relatively rare. Cystic fibrosis, the most common recessive illness, occurs in about 1 of every 2,300 children born in the United States. Using data on the incidence of a recessive genetic disease, it can be determined what percentage of the population carries a specific gene.

The chances of offspring inheriting a gene for a disorder known to be carried by their parents can also be determined. The same arithmetic that Gregor Mendel used to describe inheritance in pea plants can be applied to human recessive diseases (which is why they often are called Mendelian recessives). If two carriers of the same recessive gene have a child, there is one chance in four that the child will inherit two normal genes, one chance in four of inheriting two affected genes, and two chances in four of inheriting one normal and one abnormal gene. The disease occurs only in someone with two abnormal genes. Therefore, every child of such a couple has one chance in four of having the recessive disease. An important point is that the four-to-one odds apply to every pregnancy. The genetic dice are thrown anew every time. It is possible, with bad luck, for every child of carriers to be affected or, with good luck, for every child to escape the disease.

A 1929 photo of folk-singer Woody Guthrie. Guthrie suffered from Huntington's chorea, a dominant gene disorder that causes a slow and fatal deterioration of the nervous system. Doctors can now test people for the presence of the disease-causing gene.

SEX-LINKED DISORDERS

There is another pattern of inheritance for genetic diseases that is related to the X chromosome's size. It is much larger than is the Y chromosome and so has more genes than does the Y. If something is wrong with one of these genes, a girl has another copy, on the other X chromosome, as a backup. A boy does not. So there are sex-linked genetic diseases that occur only in males.

Hemophilia (a disease characterized by the blood's decreased ability to clot) is one such disease. Muscular dystrophy, a degenerative muscle disease, is another. The most common sex-linked disorder is *red-green color blindness*, which affects 1 of every 12 white males. In all these conditions, the gene that suffers the defect is on the X chromosome. The pattern of inheritance is that women do not have the disease but pass the affected gene on to their male offspring because a male gets his X chromosome from his mother. Men have the disease but do not pass it on to their male offspring because the Y chromosome, which determines maleness, comes from the father. They do pass the chromosome, though not necessarily the disease, on to all of their female offspring. The son of a woman carrier has a 50% chance of inheriting the affected gene and, thus, of having the disease.

ENVIRONMENTALLY INDUCED GENETIC DISORDERS

There is another large group of genetic conditions that are caused by multiple factors, often involving an interaction between genes and the environment. These conditions include *cleft palate* (a fissure in the roof of the mouth), *clubfoot* (a defect in which the foot is twisted out of shape or position), a group of disorders involving defects of the *neural tube* (the area in an embryo that develops into the brain and spinal cord), and such diseases as diabetes, various sorts of heart disease, some *allergies* (excess immune system response to foreign particles), and rheumatoid arthritis. Some of these defects are present at birth. Others appear later in life, sometimes in childhood, sometimes much later. Research has just begun to achieve an understanding of most of these conditions.

A turn-of-the-century depiction by Currier and Ives of a family of albinos. Albinism is the general name for a group of disorders affecting the pigment cells, causing a lack of color in the skin, eyes, and hair. Some types of albinism are sex-linked.

Consider neural tube defects, which affect the brain and spinal cord. One form is *anencephaly*, where all or much of the brain is absent. Another is *spina bifida*, in which the spinal column is left open and the spinal cord unprotected. Diet, geography, and time of year affect the incidence of neural tube defects. The condition is most common in babies born in autumn and winter. In Britain, which has a high incidence, there are more neural tube defects in Northern Ireland than in southern England. Vitamin supplements taken during pregnancy reduce the incidence of the condition. There is no explanation why.

There are clearly genetic factors in many common diseases, such as diabetes and rheumatoid arthritis, as well as in mental illnesses such as schizophrenia and some forms of depression. These conditions tend to run in families, yet not every member of a family will develop the condition. Because these diseases cause much suffering and death in today's society, scientists are doing a great deal of research to understand how genes and environmental factors interact to cause them.

doing a great deal of research to understand how genes and environmental factors interact to cause them.

There are powerful new tools for that research, tools that also are used in medical practice. Medical genetics is a very young field in which laboratory findings are often put directly into practical use. The next chapter will look at medical genetics.

•   •   •   •

CHAPTER 7

MEDICAL GENETICS

The modern discipline of medical genetics was born about 30 years ago. Doctors have always tried to treat patients with genetic disorders, doing whatever they could to lessen suffering and extend life. But it was not until the early 1960s, when research produced techniques for detecting genetic diseases before birth, that they could do more.

GENETIC TESTING

Several genetic tests that once might have seemed futuristic are now done routinely. Their use has been controversial, but it has given people options previously unavailable. It is possible to determine not only if a fetus carries a genetic defect but also such traits as a fetus's gender. It is conceivable that in the near future, parents could have tests done to determine eye color, hair color, and other physical characteristics as well.

Amniocentesis

The major advance in genetic testing was the development of a technique called *amniocentesis*, in which a doctor inserts a needle into the womb of a pregnant woman to obtain a sample of the *amniotic fluid* (the fluid in one of the membranes that surrounds the fetus). Obstetricians began working on amniocentesis as early as the 1930s. They moved with great caution for fear that any intrusion into the womb could cause a miscarriage. That fear proved to be exaggerated. A large number of studies on thousands of pregnancies has shown that amniocentesis, properly done, is quite safe.

The first use of amniocentesis for *prenatal* (before birth) diagnosis came in 1961, when the method was used to detect a condition called *Rh disease*, in which the fetus's blood type is incompatible with the mother's. Rh disease was once almost inevitably fatal to the fetus. Now there is a vaccine that can prevent it, and affected fetuses can be saved by blood transfusions in the womb.

The next advance was based on the discovery of the Barr body. Some cells from the fetus float in the amniotic fluid. In the early 1960s, obstetricians began looking at these cells to determine whether the fetus was male or female. This analysis can be used in pregnancies where parents are known to carry the genes for sex-linked disorders such as hemophilia or muscular dystrophy. These conditions occur only in males. If the Barr body was present, the obstetrician could assure the parents that the baby would be female and would not have the disease. If the Barr body was absent, the parents were told that the fetus was male and so had a 50% chance of having the condition. After abortion became legal in the United States in 1973, parents there had the choice of continuing the pregnancy or terminating it.

In the mid-1960s, medical geneticists began to grow fetal cells in the laboratory for more extensive analysis. The first use of this

NORMAL FEMALE
46,XX

Karyotypes for a normal female (top) and a normal male (bottom). All chromosome pairs are numbered and can be identified by their shape, size, and unique bands. If pair 23 is an XX, the person is female; if it is XY, the person is male.

NORMAL MALE
46,XY

method was made in 1968 by Carlo Valenti of New York University, who made a chromosomal map, called a *karyotype*, of the cells to detect the extra chromosome that causes Down's syndrome. Many other conditions caused by extra or missing chromosomes can be prenatally diagnosed the same way, but Down's syndrome is by far the most common of them.

The next advance was analysis of enzymes from fetal cells to determine the presence of biochemical diseases. Many of these genetic diseases are caused by the absence of a specific enzyme. A test for the enzyme can determine whether the fetus has the condition. The first biochemical condition to be diagnosed prenatally was Tay-Sachs disease, a disorder in which steady deterioration of the nervous system causes death just a few years after birth. Doctors can now detect prenatally more than 150 biochemical genetic disorders.

Chorionic Villi Sampling

The latest advance in prenatal detection is a technique for gathering fetal cells called *chorionic villi sampling*. Amniocentesis cannot be done until about the 12th week of pregnancy. Chorionic villi sampling is done much earlier, in the ninth week. If a serious defect is found and if the parents so choose, the mother can have a first trimester abortion, which is much safer and much less expensive than a second trimester abortion.

A thin *catheter* (plastic tube) is passed through the vagina and cervix, and a tiny bit of tissue is clipped off the *chorion*, another membrane surrounding the fetus. Chorionic cells are genetically identical to those of the fetus, and they can be analyzed in the same way as those gathered through amniocentesis. Chorionic villi sampling allows detection of genetic defects very early in pregnancy. But it appears to increase the risk of fetal death somewhat—just how much is hard to tell because the percentage of early pregnancies that end in spontaneous abortion or miscarriage is not known. Current studies indicate that chorionic villi sampling is almost as safe as amniocentesis, but more studies are being done to prove it.

Other Tests

A new element in prenatal testing in recent years is the discovery that levels of *alpha-fetoprotein* (AFP) in a pregnant woman's blood can indicate genetic disorders. AFP is a protein produced by the fetus. High maternal blood levels of AFP can indicate an increased risk of neural tube defects. Low levels indicate an increased risk of Down's syndrome. Because the AFP blood test is easily done, it is recommended for all pregnancies.

It is important to stress that AFP is used as a screening test. Most women with abnormal AFP blood levels bear normal babies. A high or low AFP reading is merely an indicator that further testing is needed.

The first recommended test is an *ultrasound examination*, which gives an image of the fetus in the womb. Obstetricians can estimate the age of the fetus by studying the image; they can also determine whether the woman is carrying twins or other multiple fetuses. Twins make more AFP than does one fetus, and AFP production increases as the fetus grows. Either finding can explain a high AFP level. If neither of these factors is present to explain the elevated level, amniocentesis is recommended.

Most prenatal testing is done for chromosomal disorders, usually for Down's syndrome. It is often prescribed in the case of advanced maternal age, meaning a pregnancy after the age of 34 or 35. The incidence of Down's syndrome and of other chromosomal defects increases with rising maternal age for unknown reasons, and obstetricians recommend prenatal testing for all pregnant women in their mid-thirties. Abnormal AFP levels are another reason for doing an amniocentesis. Testing is also done for couples who are known to have a chromosomal defect.

These tests are complicated and are done only in the cases mentioned or when there is a known reason—for example, birth of a previous baby with a biochemical disorder or the presence of a defective gene in prospective parents. It has become possible to test for some genes in certain populations so that couples can know in advance whether they face a potential problem. The best-known example is Tay-Sachs disease, which is prevalent in Ashkenazi Jews, or Jews of eastern European descent. Mass screening programs for carriers of the Tay-Sachs gene have been carried out in several cities.

This sort of specific testing is possible only for a minority of genetic disorders, those in which the biochemical abnormality has been clearly identified. Medical geneticists like to talk about the several dozen conditions in which the biochemical defect—

the missing or abnormal enzyme—is known. They are frustrated by the many more conditions in which the cause of the problem still has not been identified and prenatal screening by biochemical tests is not possible. In just the past few years, a new biomedical technology has made it possible to diagnose some previously undiagnosable disorders in some families.

The best diagnostic test is one that detects the gene responsible for a disease. Next best is a test that detects the faulty enzyme produced by that gene. But most defective genes and faulty enzymes are hard to find. So scientists have turned to the next best thing, detection of a normal gene that travels along with the disease-causing gene.

Genetic Markers

Many normal genes come in a number of varieties, or different alleles. Alleles of the same gene produce enzymes that do the same job, but the alleles can be distinguished because their nucleotide sequences are slightly different. So geneticists look for an allele of a normal gene that passes from generation to generation along with the gene that causes a disease. They use that gene as a *marker*. The technique is possible if the geneticist can find (1) a readily detectable marker gene that has a number of alleles and (2) a family in which the disease occurs and whose members carry several alleles of the marker gene.

The search for marker genes is made possible by restriction enzymes. Each restriction enzyme cuts DNA at a site where a certain nucleotide sequence occurs; the site is different for each restriction enzyme. No two individuals have the same DNA sequences because of all the variations that occur when chromosomes are reproduced. The differences are called *polymorphisms*, distinctive patterns of fragments, which differ for each person. Those fragments have been given a marvelously recondite name: *restriction-fragment-length polymorphisms*, or RFLPs, pronounced "riflips."

When geneticists do a search, they extract DNA from cells, expose them to restriction enzymes, and put the fragments in a viscous substance through which is run an electric current that pulls the fragments apart. A technique called *Southern blotting* (named for a Scot, Edward Southern) picks out the fragments of interest, those that bear the marker gene. A Southern blot uses radioactive DNA segments that bind to the marker gene. After more manipulation, the geneticist has a RFLP that carries the marker gene and, presumably, the flawed gene.

This work can get tricky because markers do not always go right along with the defective gene. Some marker genes are near the disease gene, some are farther away, so the odds that the 2 go together are not 100%. And a marker can be identified only if it is tracked through several generations of a family in which the disease occurs. A gene becomes a marker if one allele is found in family members who have the disease but not in those who do not have the disease. The first condition in which the RFLP technique was used successfully to find a marker was *Duchenne type muscular dystrophy*, a sex-linked disorder. Knowledge that the gene is on the X chromosome made the search easier.

The gene for Huntington's chorea was next. In 1983, a team headed by James Gusella of Harvard Medical School looked at

Martin Cline, a doctor at UCLA Medical Center, headed a team that inserted a new gene into this mouse. This procedure may play a significant role in cancer research and in the development of gene therapy to treat such diseases as sickle-cell anemia.

eight marker genes in a large Venezuelan family before finding one that was linked to the disease. The gene is now known to be on chromosome 4. Markers have since been found for genes for cystic fibrosis, some forms of manic depression, and a number of other diseases.

Once a marker is found, people suspected of carrying the gene for the disease can be tested for it. If someone carries the marker—the specific allele linked to the gene for the disease— the odds that the disease gene is present can be calculated. The odds are hardly ever 100%. They depend on the distance between the marker gene and the gene for the disease. The smaller the distance, the larger the odds that the disease gene has not been separated from the marker gene by crossing-over or some other error of DNA reproduction. But with a good marker, geneticists can be more than 90% certain about the predictions they make.

Finding a marker is an essential step toward locating the actual gene, which is a major goal of geneticists. Once the gene is found, its nucleotide sequence can be determined. The normal and defective versions of the gene (and of the protein it encodes) can be compared to learn the biochemical nature of the disease, a step toward treatment and cure. In the case of Duchenne type muscular dystrophy, Dr. Louis Kunkel, of Harvard Medical School, and his collaborators identified in 1988 a missing portion of the X chromosome in patients. That portion of the chromosome contained the gene, which has been isolated and cloned. A widely used technique is *chromosome walking*—finding a restriction fragment that matches the end of the marker gene, then finding a fragment that matches the end of that fragment, and so on until the gene itself is reached.

GENE THERAPY

The ultimate goal of the search for a flawed gene is treatment of the disease by *gene therapy*—replacement of a defective gene by a normal one. In theory, the tools for gene therapy are already at hand. Genetic engineering of animals and plants by insertion of genes is already proceeding in many laboratories. In practice, gene therapy in humans has proved to be much more difficult than had been expected.

Several techniques for gene therapy have been tested. The most promising uses a retrovirus that is first made harmless and then has the appropriate gene inserted into its DNA. A laboratory culture of human cells containing the flawed gene is infected with the retrovirus. Doctors then inject the patient with cells in which the normal gene takes root and produces its protein, and (it is hoped) the injection will correct the genetic flaw that causes the diseases.

One problem that emerged in experimental work was the difficulty of implanting the gene in the proper location. Only a very small percentage of infected cells had adequate protein production. For example, Randall Willis and colleagues at the University of California at San Diego, in 1985, inserted a normal gene into laboratory cultures of blood cells to correct the genetic flaw of *Lesch-Nyhan disease* (a neurological condition), but the inserted gene produced very low levels of the normal enzyme.

Once the genetic flaw is corrected in individual cells, a second problem is getting those cells to the proper location in the body.

Born with SCID, this 11-month-old boy has received a bone marrow transplant. Transplanting genetically altered bone marrow cells may be an effective treatment for SCID.

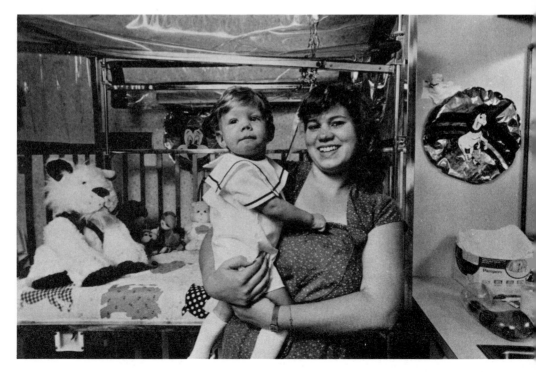

For example, the corrected gene for Lesch-Nyhan disease most likely would have to be implanted in the delicate nerve cells of the brain, an extremely difficult task.

The most likely candidate for the first attempt at human gene therapy is a condition called *severe combined immunodeficiency* (SCID) whose victims are born without immune defenses because their bone marrow cells, the precursors of certain immune cells, are genetically deficient. Untreated SCID patients die quickly as their body is overwhelmed by infections. They might be cured by implantation of genetically altered bone marrow cells. A similar experiment, done on cancer patients, was recently delayed not only by technological problems but also by ethical and moral considerations about the wisdom of applying genetic engineering techniques to human beings.

In 1988, the NIH was asked to consider a proposal that would allow a group led by W. Anderson French of the National Heart, Lung, and Blood Institute and Steven Rosenberg and R. Michael Blaese of the National Cancer Institute to inject genetically engineered white blood cells into a small number of cancer patients undergoing an experimental treatment.

In the treatment, white blood cells are removed from the patients and treated with *interleukin-2*, an immune system molecule that strengthens the cells' ability to kill cancer cells. Only half the patients receiving the treatment benefit from it. The NIH researchers wanted to implant a harmless marker gene into the treated white cells to study their fate in each patient. The object was to identify the patients who benefit from the treatment. The NIH hesitated and studied the project for months before allowing it to proceed in 1989.

Such advances in medical genetics are made possible by basic research. The tools of molecular biology have become increasingly powerful, and genes are now being mapped, cloned, and studied routinely.

•   •   •   •

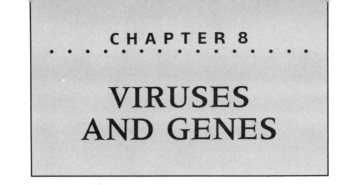

CHAPTER 8
. . . .
VIRUSES
AND GENES

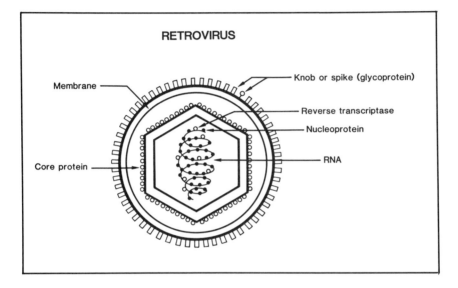

RETROVIRUS

Membrane

Knob or spike (glycoprotein)

Reverse transcriptase

Nucleoprotein

Core protein

RNA

Viruses used to be described simply as cellular parasites, which do nothing but cause harm. Now it has become apparent that they are more than just disease agents. Some of them appear to be central actors in genetics and evolution. They transfer genes from cell to cell in ways that biologists are just beginning to understand.

VIRUSES AND CANCER

A lot of what is known about viruses comes from cancer research. The belief that some viruses can cause cancer has been around for a long time. In the late 1960s, George Todaro and Robert

Huebner of the National Cancer Institute coined the term *oncogene*. They believed that oncogenes were potentially dangerous passengers in human chromosomes, possibly planted there early in life by viruses. The oncogenes usually remained inactive, but they would make cells cancerous when stimulated into activity by *carcinogens* (cancer-causing agents) such as certain chemicals.

For years, Todaro, Huebner, and many other scientists tried to identify a human oncogene, but without success. There were many claims that a human oncogene had been found in the 1970s. None of them proved true.

The stalemate was broken through studies of a well-known retrovirus that causes a form of cancer called *sarcoma* in chickens. (A retrovirus has RNA rather than DNA as its genetic ma-

In 1910, Francis Peyton Rous discovered a virus that causes a type of cancer in chickens. Rous's finding was so revolutionary and controversial that it was not until 1966 that he won the Nobel Prize in physiology or medicine for his cancer research.

terial, and an enzyme called reverse transcriptase translates RNA into DNA.) The existence of the chicken sarcoma virus was discovered in 1910 by Francis Peyton Rous, a researcher at the Rockefeller Institute. It aroused such disbelief that Rous gave up the study. Eventually, the evidence that viruses cause cancer in animals became overwhelming. Rous (with Charles Brenton Huggins) won the Nobel Prize in physiology or medicine in 1966, when he was 87 years old.

In the 1970s, it was found that if the Rous sarcoma virus grows in the laboratory for a long time, mutants can emerge that no longer cause cancer. Scientists traced the difference to a small gene, about 1,000 nucleotides long, found only in the cancer-causing form of the virus. They called the gene *src*, an abbreviation for sarcoma.

In the next few years, similar oncogenes were found in a number of other retroviruses that cause cancer in species of birds and mammals. By custom, oncogenes are given three-letter names according to the species in which they are found: *ras* for the rat sarcoma virus, *fes* for the feline (cat) sarcoma virus, and so on. In all, several dozen oncogenes have been discovered.

In every case, the virus could get along well without the oncogene, which suggested that the oncogenes had originated outside the virus. That suspicion was confirmed in the mid-1970s when Michael Bishop and Harold Varmus of the University of California at San Francisco found that the src virus was present in normal noncancerous chicken cells. They called the version of the src gene found in cells a *proto-oncogene*, to distinguish it from the oncogenes retroviruses carry. Other researchers found that for every viral oncogene, there is a cellular proto-oncogene.

In the language of science, proto-oncogenes are said to be highly conserved, meaning that they are present in species ranging from the most primitive, such as yeast, to the most advanced. It is assumed that a highly conserved gene makes a protein necessary for some basic function that every cell needs to survive, grow, or reproduce. Cancer is uncontrolled cell growth. A cancerous cell has somehow lost the controls that make normal cells reproduce just enough at just the right time. The sum of these observations led to the working hypothesis that an oncogene is just a normal gene gone wrong, often with the help of a retrovirus.

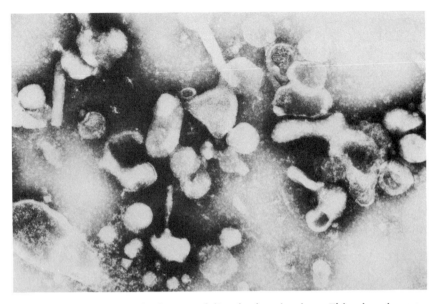

An electron micrograph shows a feline leukemia virus. This virus is one of the many retroviruses that cause normal cells to turn malignant in animals.

The hypothesis is that a virus picks up a proto-oncogene from one cell and transports it to another. The transported gene integrates itself in the DNA of the new cell and goes to work. Something in what it does leads a normal cell to become cancerous.

All of these theories came from work done with animal viruses. A major new development occurred in the early 1980s, when proto-oncogenes were found in human cancer cells. Most of the proto-oncogenes isolated from human cancer cells were similar or identical to animal viral oncogenes, although those viruses did not cause cancer in humans. Further studies showed that normal cells contain the same proto-oncogenes.

But researchers still did not have a clue about what these genes did in the cell. The first understanding came from studies of a protein called *platelet-derived growth factor* (PDGF). Growth factors are substances produced in the body that promote multiplication of cells. In 1983, Michael Waterfield and his colleagues at the Imperial Cancer Research Fund in London worked out the molecular sequence of PDGF. When they fed it into a computer data base listing all known proteins, they found it identical with the protein made by an oncogene called *sis*, first isolated from the simian (monkey) sarcoma virus.

That stood to reason. Cancer is uncontrolled multiplication of cells, so it was no surprise to find that a substance that stimulates cell multiplication is involved. The proteins made by a number of other oncogenes have since been identified. Many are growth factors. Others play important roles in the rapid growth and development that occurs early in life. An activity that was beneficial at the right time in life became malignant when it occurred at an inappropriate time. The question was, What made these oncogenes go wrong?

Sparking Cancer

There are at least three possibilities for what might spark a cell to turn cancerous. One is that the event is triggered by a mutated version of the gene. Another is that the gene becomes overactive. A third is that it gets turned on at the wrong time because of a chromosomal abnormality. So far, all three possibilities seem to be true, for different oncogenes.

In a study of the proto-oncogene ras, Robert Weinberg of MIT found that the ras protein made by cancerous cells differed by a single amino acid from the protein in normal cells. There was a point mutation that caused the amino acid valine to be substituted for glycine.

Looking at cells from *Burkitt's lymphoma*, a cancer common in Africa, researchers found a chromosomal translocation in which material migrated from chromosome 8 to chromosome 14. That migration, they found, put the myc proto-oncogene next to a segment of DNA that regulates gene activation. The belief is that the change causes the myc gene to overproduce its protein, transforming the cell from normal to malignant.

Looking at oncogenes in retroviruses, researchers at Rockefeller University found that these oncogenes were flanked by stretches of DNA that promote gene activity. These promoters are obviously useful when a virus invades a cell because they ensure that the viral genes will be more active than the cell's own genes, thus helping the virus to reproduce. If they happen to promote the activity of an oncogene, that can help turn a cell cancerous.

One can ask why a proto-oncogene from a normal cell should turn up in a virus. There is no definite answer, but there are some good clues. Scientists know that retroviruses have RNA as their genetic material. They also know that cells contain lots of RNA, including messenger RNA sequences that carry the genetic sequences of genes. When a virus enters a cell, its only task is to make many copies of itself. It is logical to assume that the copying is not perfect and that somewhere along the line the RNA for a proto-oncogene gets included in copies of the virus, which go on to invade other cells.

It is also logical to assume that the RNA for other genes also gets carried from cell to cell by retroviruses. Researchers zeroed in on oncogenes because of a passionate interest in the genetics of cancer. They first thought they had found a unique family of genes. Now they know that proto-oncogenes are not unique but instead are part of any cell's normal genetic apparatus. Therefore, it is probable that other normal cells having nothing to do with cancer undergo the same gene transfer. If viruses transfer genes between species, as seems possible, then they may play an important role in evolution—a possibility that geneticists are just beginning to explore.

As for cancer, the role of oncogenes is more complicated than was first believed. An early hope was that research could identify a single genetic event that turned a normal cell cancerous. If that event were stopped, cancer could be prevented. It has now been established that more than one oncogene is involved in malignant transformation. For example, Robert Weinberg's group at MIT has shown that both the myc and ras oncogenes are needed to turn cells malignant in culture. Bert Vogelstein at Johns Hopkins University has shown that perhaps five genetic events must occur to cause colon cancer. Scientists speak of a *genetic cascade* leading to malignancy.

Some of those steps include a newly discovered kind of gene called an *anti-oncogene*. It is the absence, not the presence, of an anti-oncogene that leads to cancerous transformation. Evidence for the existence of anti-oncogenes was first found in patients with *retinoblastoma*, an inherited form of eye cancer. In

1986, Webster Cavenee of the University of Cincinnati found a deletion that inactivated a gene on one chromosome. Inactivation of the same gene on the other chromosome led to cancerous transformation. The same gene defect has been found in patients with lung cancer, breast cancer, and a bone cancer called *osteosarcoma*; scientists are looking for it in other cancers as well. As these words are written, researchers do not know how absence of the anti-oncogene leads to cancer, but they are working hard to find out. The best hypothesis at the moment is that it inhibits cell growth, perhaps shutting down the growth factor proto-oncogenes.

Geneticists could make more progress toward understanding cancer if they knew the exact location and nucleotide sequence of oncogenes and anti-oncogenes. The same is true of many other

Robert A. Weinberg (right) and Salvador E. Luria, director of the MIT Center for Cancer Research. Weinberg and his colleagues have shown that more than one oncogene is needed to turn cells malignant.

genetic diseases. Many human genes have been mapped and sequenced, and the pace of the work is quickening, but progress is not fast enough to satisfy many biologists. They have proposed a major international program to map and sequence the entire *human genome*—all the genes in the human cell—over a 10-year period.

•   •   •   •

CHAPTER 9
· · · · · · · · · · · · · · ·

MAPPING THE HUMAN GENOME

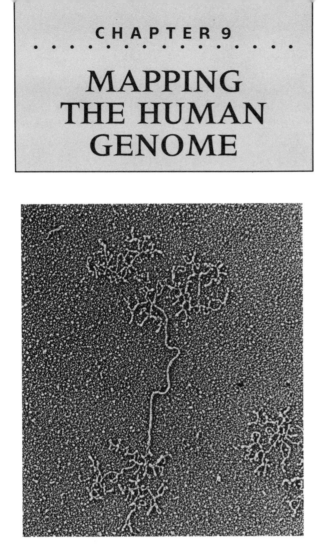

Electron micrograph of a pure gene magnified 79,300 times

The human genome project has two elements. One is development of a genetic map, a set of markers for all 23 pairs of chromosomes that would allow geneticists to determine the exact location of all the human genes, estimated to number between 50,000 and 100,000. The other is sequencing of the genome, working out the exact sequence of the estimated 3 billion nucleotides in all the human chromosomes.

Both efforts are already under way in a coordinated effort involving dozens of laboratories. Human gene maps of a sort already exist. Segments of some chromosomes have been sequenced. This chapter will first look at the methods of gene mapping and sequencing, then discuss why scientists think it important to increase the pace of the work.

EARLY GENE MAPS

The first gene to be mapped was the one for color blindness. In 1911, E. B. Wilson, working at Columbia University, noticed that only males were color-blind and concluded that the gene had to be on the X chromosome. Genes for a few dozen other sex-linked conditions, hemophilia and Duchenne type muscular dystrophy among them, were mapped to the X chromosome over the next few decades.

Progress was slow until the 1960s, when Mary C. Weiss and Howard Green at New York University developed a technique of fusing human skin cells and mouse cells in a laboratory dish. The human chromosomes in colonies of these hybrid cells tended to die out as they reproduced, often leaving only a single chromosome. That chromosome can be identified by exposing it to a fluorescent dye. Each pair of human chromosomes (numbered 1 to 22, plus the X and Y sex chromosomes) can be distinguished by its distinctive pattern of bands. If the researchers could identify a human protein being produced by the fused mouse/human cell, they could say that the gene for the protein was on the last remaining chromosome. A number of genes were mapped to specific chromosomes by this method.

But saying that a gene—or two or three—is on a chromosome is a very primitive form of mapping. Scientists want to know at least the location of the gene relative to other genes on the chromosome. The cell-fusion method made that sort of mapping possible. In some hybrid cells, only a fragment of a human chromosome survived. If such a cell produced a human protein, the gene for that protein was obviously on that fragment. By studying various fragments and the proteins they produced, researchers were able to map dozens of genes to specific chromosomes and work out the order of the genes on a chromosome.

More genes were mapped by other methods. In 1968, for example, researchers at Johns Hopkins University assigned the gene for the so-called *Duffy blood type* to chromosome 1 by studying a family in which that blood type occurred. Family members who had the Duffy blood type had an identifiable variation of chromosome 1 that was not present in members who had a different blood type. Such linkages were used to map a number of other genes.

The great leap forward in gene mapping came with the discovery of restriction enzymes, which cut DNA at known locations. It has been found that exposing DNA of different individuals to restriction enzymes produces fragments of different lengths, the RFLPs mentioned in Chapter 7. In 1980, David Botstein of MIT, Raymond White and Mark Skolnik of the University of Utah, and Ronald Davis of Stanford University suggested that RFLPs could be used to produce a genetic map. Their idea was to find a regularly spaced set of genetic markers, genes that could easily be picked out along each chromosome. Those marker genes could then be used to fix the location of other genes.

MAPPING TECHNIQUES

The mapping principle is as simple as going into uncharted country and hammering a series of numbered stakes into the ground at set intervals. The location of a house or farm can be designated by its distance from the nearest stake. Mapping a chromosome is simpler in one respect than mapping land because only one dimension has to be considered—length along the DNA molecule. It is more difficult because the markers provided by nature are somewhat irregular. The RFLP method of mapping is based on the frequent occurrence of polymorphisms—differences in nucleotide sequence—in chromosomes of different individuals. On the average, there is a difference in sequence every 200 to 500 base pairs. Cutting chromosomes with restriction enzymes thus produces different patterns of fragments that, with proper processing, can be used as markers. The mapper uses a *DNA probe*, a segment of DNA of known sequence, to pick out an identifiable RFLP. The probe and the RFLP are used as a reference point on the chromosome. A complete map consists of a large number of evenly spaced markers on all the chromosomes.

The technique works best with a large family whose members volunteer to give blood samples so RFLPs can be followed through several generations.

The completion of two genetic maps was announced in 1987. One was developed by Collaborative Research, a genetic engineering company in Massachusetts. The other was developed by Raymond White and his collaborators, who worked with three generations of a Mormon family in Utah. Each map has several hundred markers. The most complete section of White's map has 475 markers covering 17 of the 23 human chromosome pairs. The Collaborative Research map has 403 markers. The spacing in each is a marker every 10 to 20 million nucleotides. Higher-resolution maps are being prepared.

A newer method of gene mapping is based on the existence of long, repeated sequences of DNA at many sites in the human genome. The origin and function of these *tandem repeats* are not known. The advantage they offer for mapping is that the number of repeats of a given sequence varies greatly in the population. Cutting DNA with restriction enzymes thus produces distinctive patterns of fragments that can be used as markers. Use of *variable-number tandem repeats* (VNTRs) makes possible a genetic map with markers only 1 million nucleotides apart. Such a map will have more than 3,000 markers for the human genome.

USES OF MAPS

VNTRs can be used as genetic fingerprints, a discovery made in 1985 by Alec Jeffreys of the University of Leicester in England. Jeffreys recognized that VNTRs are as distinctive as fingerprints and in some ways more useful. DNA obtained from blood or semen can be used to determine whether a suspect was at the scene of a crime. DNA obtained from cells can be used to determine parentage. DNA fingerprinting is rapidly gaining secure legal status. In fact, the first murder conviction in the United States to use DNA fingerprinting occurred in Richmond, Virginia, in September 1989.

Very small samples of DNA can be analyzed by a technique called *gene amplification*, devised in the 1980s by Kary Mullis and colleagues at the Cetus Corporation in California. Gene amplification is done by binding *primers*, short sequences of DNA, to either side of the segment that is to be amplified. The enzyme DNA polymerase is then used to make multiple copies of the sequence. Millions of copies of a DNA sequence can be produced in a matter of hours.

Genetic mapping information gathered by all the techniques is kept at a Paris-based organization, the Center for the Study of Human Polymorphism (known as CEPH for its French name). CEPH ships DNA probes to geneticists all over the world, who are obliged in turn to send the data they gather to CEPH. As data accumulate, the number of markers and of genes whose location is known increases at a faster pace. As of 1989, human genes were being mapped at better than two a week, and that rate was increasing.

Helen Donis-Keller, senior researcher on a four-year genetic mapping project (right), and Philip Green in a 1987 photo taken at Collaborative Research, a Massachussetts genetic engineering company, where their research group has compiled the first detailed map of "signposts" in the human genome.

SEQUENCING DNA

Sequencing, the other part of the human genome project, is somewhat controversial. Like mapping, sequencing is an ongoing effort of many laboratories. The two basic methods of sequencing were developed in the 1970s by Walter Gilbert and Allan Maxam at Harvard and Walter Sanger at Cambridge University in England. Sanger's method is to separate a number of strands of a specific segment of DNA and break copies of one strand into multiple, overlapping fragments. The nucleotide sequence of each fragment is determined, and the overall sequence of the entire segment is found by fitting the overlapping pieces together. The Gilbert-Maxam method is essentially the same but uses a different method of breaking the DNA into fragments.

Sequencing is tedious work. One scientist working for 1 year can sequence a DNA segment of about 50,000 nucleotides, the size of a large gene, at a cost of about $1 per nucleotide. That would make the cost of sequencing the entire human genome about $3 billion. Leroy Hood of the California Institute of Technology has invented an automated DNA sequencer that can do about 10,000 bases a day. He says improved automation could bring the cost of sequencing down to 10 cents a nucleotide, which would be $300 million for the entire genome.

The controversy about sequencing arises from fears that its high cost would take funds away from other fields of biology and would introduce a mammoth bureaucracy of a kind that most biologists detest. There are also questions about the value of a complete sequence. No two human genomes are alike because of chromosomal crossing-over and other errors of gene replication. Should the genome of one individual be sequenced? Should scientists use a composite of chromosomes from many individuals? There are no answers yet, but one proposal is to sequence one of the samples maintained at CEPH in Paris and later to sequence several other human genomes as well.

Critics of a sequencing crash program also point out that most of the genome consists not of active genes but of tandem repeats, introns that are snipped out when a gene is expressed, and other "silent regions" of DNA. It is not clear whether these regions, which make up the great majority of the genome, are worth sequencing. Some biologists say they are just nonsense sequences. Others say the silent regions could have important functions that will be learned only if their sequences become known.

The issue is not really whether the human genome will be mapped and sequenced, because steady progress is being made in both efforts. The question is whether the process should be speeded up by a major infusion of funds and the formation of a coordinated international effort. The consensus is that a speedier effort is worth the money, but there is some dissent.

THE FUTURE

Scientists agree that a complete gene map and sequence will be of enormous help medically and scientifically. A map will allow geneticists to find more of the estimated 4,000 gene defects that cause genetic diseases. A sequence data bank will help clarify the role of various genes in illness and health. Examples already are

A scientist from the Human Genome Center works on a computer-controlled robot that hastens the mapping of the human genome.

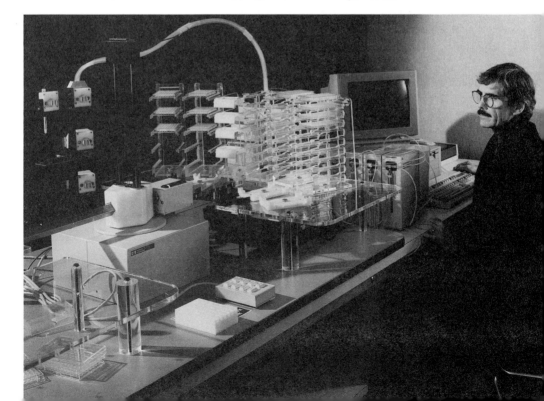

at hand. Location of the genes for Huntington's chorea and muscular dystrophy was made possible by gene mapping. And computerized sequence data bases such as GenBank, maintained at Los Alamos National Laboratory, enabled scientists to learn that oncogenes have an essential role in normal growth and development.

So the plus side of the human genome project is help for patients with genetic diseases and possible progress against cancer, diabetes, and other illnesses. The minus side arises from growing knowledge that some genes make individuals more likely to develop disorders such as schizophrenia, cancer, heart disease, and some forms of depression. Genetics clearly plays a role in these and many other diseases. Those who support the human genome project say that more knowledge about the interplay of genes and environmental factors can help prevent illness in individuals who are found to have a genetic vulnerability to one condition or another. Critics note that there is a serious possibility of misuse of such genetic information. They say, for example, that corporations may someday demand genetic testing and refuse to hire individuals who carry certain genes. Criticism of the human genome project has been strongest in Europe, where there are powerful memories of Nazi Germany's systematic extermination of people who were described as genetically inferior by Adolf Hitler's twisted thinking.

The debate is necessary because genetic research will go on. Mapping and sequencing will continue whether there is an official human genome project or not. People have entered a time in which biologists have unparalleled knowledge of their genetic inheritance and powerful tools for manipulating it. The challenge is to ensure that this information will be used wisely.

•   •   •   •

APPENDIX:
FOR MORE INFORMATION

The following organizations can provide further information on genetic counseling.

GENERAL

March of Dimes Birth Defects
  Foundation
1275 Mamaroneck Avenue
White Plains, NY 10605
(914) 428-7100
(provides information; also refers
  individuals to local genetic
  counseling services)

National Genetics Foundation
555 West 57th Street
New York, NY 10019
(212) 586-5800
(offers computerized analysis of

individual's family health history;
  also operates a national
  clearinghouse staffed by genetic
  counselors who refer individuals
  to local genetic centers)

National Maternal and Child Health
  Clearinghouse
3520 Prospect Street NW
Washington, DC 20057
(202) 625-8410
(provides pamphlets and booklets
  on various genetic disorders and
  counseling services)

The following is a list of organizations in the United States and Canada that provide further information on various genetic diseases and disorders.

CYSTIC FIBROSIS

Canadian Cystic Fibrosis
  Foundation
2221 Yonge Street
Suite 601
Toronto, Ontario M4S 2B4
Canada
(416) 485-9149

Cystic Fibrosis Foundation
#200
6931 Arlington Road
Bethesda, MD 20814
(301) 951-4422

HUNTINGTON'S CHOREA

Huntington's Disease Society of
America
140 West 22nd Street
6th Floor
New York, NY 10011
(212) 757-0443

Huntington Society of Canada
13 Water Street North
Suite 3
P.O. Box 333
Cambridge, Ontario N1R 5T8
Canada
(519) 622-1002

National Huntington's Disease
Association
1182 Broadway
Suite 402
New York, NY 10001
(212) 684-2781

MUSCULAR DYSTROPHY

Muscular Dystrophy Association
810 Seventh Avenue
New York, NY 10019
(212) 586-0808

Muscular Dystrophy Association of
Canada
150 Eglinton Avenue East
Suite 400
Toronto, Ontario M4P 1E8
Canada
(416) 488-0030

SICKLE-CELL ANEMIA

Canadian Sickle Cell Society
1801 Eglinton Avenue West
Suite 204A
Toronto, Ontario M6E 2H8
Canada
(416) 789-7615

National Association for Sickle Cell
Disease
Hot Line:
(800) 421-8453
Sickle Cell Disease Branch
Division of Blood Diseases and
Resources
National Heart, Lung, and Blood
Institute
Bethesda, MD 20892
(301) 496-6931

SPINA BIFIDA

Spina Bifida Association of America
343 South Dearborn Street
Chicago, IL 60604
(312) 663-1562
(800) 621-3141

Spina Bifida Association of Canada
633 Wellington Crescent
Winnipeg, Manitoba R3M 0A8
Canada
(204) 452-7580

TAY-SACHS DISEASE

National Tay-Sachs & Allied
Diseases Association
92 Washington Avenue
Cedarhurst, NY 11516
(516) 569-4300

FURTHER READING

GENERAL

Arnold, Caroline. *Genetics: From Mendel to Gene Splicing*. New York: Watts, 1986.

Bornstein, Sandy, and Jerry Bornstein. *New Frontiers in Genetics*. New York: Messner, 1984.

Crick, Francis. *What Mad Pursuit: A Personal View of Scientific Discovery*. New York: Basic Books, 1988.

Fichter, George S. *Cells*. New York: Watts, 1986.

Frankel, Edward. *DNA: The Ladder of Life*. 2nd ed. New York: McGraw-Hill, 1979.

Gribbin, John. *In Search of the Double Helix: Quantum Physics and Life*. New York: Bantam Books, 1987.

Iltis, Hugo. *Life of Mendel*. London: Allen & Unwin, 1932.

Keller, Evelyn Fox. *A Feeling for the Organism*. San Francisco: Freeman, 1983.

McCarty, Maclyn. *The Transforming Principle: Discovering that Genes Are Made of DNA*. New York: Norton, 1985.

Sayre, Anne. *Rosalind Franklin & DNA*. New York: Norton, 1978.

Stent, Gunther. *The Double Helix*. London: Weidenfeld and Nicolson, 1981.

Thomas, Lewis. *The Lives of a Cell: Notes of a Biology Watcher*. New York: Penguin, 1984.

Watson, James. *Molecular Biology of the Gene*. 3rd ed. Menlo Park, CA: W. A. Benjamin, 1976.

Wilcox, Frank H. *DNA: The Thread of Life*. Minneapolis: Lerner, 1988.

EVOLUTION

Bendall, D. S. *Evolution from Molecules to Men*. New York: Cambridge University Press, 1983.

Brent, Peter. *Charles Darwin*. London: Heinemann, 1981.

Dawkins, Richard. *The Selfish Gene*. New York: Oxford University Press, 1976.

Edey, Maitland A., and Donald C. Johanson. *Blueprints, Solving the Mystery of Evolution*. Boston: Little, Brown, 1989.

Gould, Stephen Jay. *Hen's Teeth and Horse's Toes: Further Reflections in Natural History*. New York: Norton, 1983.

———. *The Panda's Thumb: More Reflections in Natural History*. New York: Norton, 1980.

McKinney, H. L. *Lamarck to Darwin: Contributions to Evolutionary Biology 1809–1859*. Lawrence, KN: Cornada Press, 1971.

Patterson, Colin. *Molecules and Morphology in Evolution: Conflict or Compromise?* New York: Cambridge University Press, 1987.

Stebbins, G. Ledyard. *Darwin to DNA: Molecules to Humanity*. San Francisco: Freeman, 1982.

GENETIC ENGINEERING

Bains, William. *Genetic Engineering for Almost Everybody*. New York: Penguin, 1988.

Milunsky, Aubrey. *Choices Not Chances: Controlling Your Genetic Heritage*. Boston: Little, Brown, 1989.

National Research Council. *Mapping and Sequencing the Human Genome*. Washington, DC: National Academy Press, 1988.

Prentis, Steve. *Biotechnology*. London: Orbis, 1984.

Rogers, Michael. *Biohazard*. New York: Knopf, 1977.

Watson, James, John Touze, and David Kurtz. *Recombinant DNA*. New York: Scientific American Books, 1983.

MEDICAL GENETICS

Berg, Kare. *Genetic Damage in Man Caused by Environmental Agents*. New York: Academic Press, 1979.

———. *Medical Genetics: Past, Present, Future*. New York: Alan R. Liss, 1985.

Bishop, J. Michael. *Genes and Cancer*. New York: Alan R. Liss, 1985.

Carter, Thomas P., and Ann M. Willey. *Genetic Disease: Screening and Management*. New York: Alan R. Liss, 1986.

McKusick, Victor A. *Medical and Experimental Mammalian Genetics: A Perspective.* New York: Alan R. Liss, 1987.

Milunsky, Aubrey. *Genetic Disorders and the Fetus: Diagnosis, Prevention, and Treatment.* 2nd ed. New York: Plenum, 1986.

Roberts, J. A., and M. E. Pembrey. *Introduction to Medical Genetics.* 8th ed. New York: Oxford University Press, 1985.

Thompson, J., and Margaret Thompson. *Genetics in Medicine.* 4th ed. Philadelphia: Saunders, 1986.

PICTURE CREDITS

GLOSSARY

AFP alpha-fetoprotein; a fetal protein; abnormally high or low levels, which can be detected in a pregnant woman's blood, may indicate certain birth defects or increased risk of pregnancy complications

allele one of two or more alternative gene forms for specific inheritable characteristics that occupy certain positions on paired chromosomes

amino acids a number of organic compounds containing an amino group and a carboxyl group; the units that make up protein

amniocentesis a test for genetic defects in an unborn child; chromosomes in fetal cells drawn from fluid inside the amnion (one of the membranes surrounding the fetus) are examined for abnormality

antibody one of the several types of protein produced by the body to combat bacteria, viruses, or other foreign substances

antigen a bacteria, virus, or other foreign substance that causes the body to form an antibody

atom the smallest unit an element can be reduced to and still retain the distinctive properties of that element

bacteria unicellular organisms that lack a distinct nuclear membrane

B cells B lymphocytes; white blood cells that produce antibodies and work in conjunction with T cells

cancer any malignant tumor that, as it moves to adjacent tissue layers or to other parts of the body, destroys normal tissue; a group of more than 100 separate diseases

cell the basic unit of all organisms; the smallest living unit that can grow, feed, and reproduce independently

chloroplasts small rounded green bodies found in the cells of leaves and stems of plants; important in the process of photosynthesis; contain their own DNA

chorionic villi sampling method of testing for genetic defects very early in a pregnancy; the chromosomes in cells taken from the chorion (one of the membranes surrounding the embryo) are examined for abnormality

chromosomes the rodlike structures found in the nucleus of mammalian cells that contain genes; each normal human cell (except gametes) contains 23 pairs of chromosomes

chromosome walking a technique for isolating a gene in which a restriction fragment that matches the end of a marker gene is found, then a fragment that matches the end of that fragment is found, and so on until the gene itself is reached

crossing-over the mutual interchange of blocks of genes between two paired chromosomes

DNA deoxyribonucleic acid; genetic material, composed of paired nitrogenous bases, that contains chemical instructions for determining an organism's inherited characteristics; found in the nucleus of eukaryotic cells

enzyme a member of a group of proteins that can facilitate or trigger (catalyze) certain chemical reactions or biological processes

gene complex unit of chemical material contained within the chromosomes; variations in the patterns formed by the components of genes are responsible for inherited traits; may be dominant (expressed if one or both alleles is dominant) or recessive (only expressed when both alleles are recessive)

gene amplification process used to study a very small segment of DNA; primers are attached to the segment and multiple copies of the DNA sequence are made

gene pool the totality of genes possessed by a population

gene therapy replacement of a defective gene by a normal one

genetic drift a chance variation, such as the likelihood of a mutant gene entering a population's gene pool; the smaller the population, the greater the chance for variation

genetic engineering artificial manipulation of segments of DNA from one organism into the DNA of another organism or addition of synthesized DNA into an organism; permits isolating and examining the properties and actions of specific genes

genetic marker a usually dominant gene used to study distribution of genes in a population and to identify gene linkage

genome the complete set of genes of an organism

hormone a product of the endocrine glands that circulates throughout the bloodstream, controlling and regulating other glands and organs

karyotype a photomicrograph of the chromosomes of a single cell in the metaphase stage of division; arranged to show the chromosomes in descending order

meiosis cell division to create gametes (sperm or ova); successive divisions of the nucleus produce cells containing half the number of chromosomes present in other cells

mitochondria small rounded organelles found in the cytoplasm of cells that produce energy for the cell; contain their own DNA

mitosis cell division of somatic cells in which each daughter cell contains the same number of chromosomes as did the parent cell

mutation permanent, inheritable change in genetic material; occurs naturally or can be caused by such external means as radiation; includes chromosomal mutations (e.g., deletion, duplication, inversion, translocation, nondisjunction, and crossing-over) and gene mutation (e.g., point mutation)

natural selection Darwin's theory of the evolution of species; natural competition for food between individual animals of a species is won by those with slight variations that make them better able to obtain food and survive to reproduce, passing on favorable genetic variation to offspring; cumulative inheritance of these variations leads to the creation of a new species

nucleotide structural unit of a nucleic acid; composed of a nitrogenous base (purine or pyrimidine), a sugar (ribose or deoxyribose), and a phosphate group

nucleus area in a cell in which genetic material is found; essential agent in growth and reproduction of a cell; in plant and animal cells the nucleus is enclosed in a membrane

oncogene a gene that is involved in the process that transforms a normal cell into a cancerous one

plasmids small separate loops of bacterial DNA; can be transferred among bacteria

primer a short sequence of DNA used in gene amplification to enlarge the segment of DNA to be studied enough to reproduce it many times

protein one of many complex molecules composed of amino acids; necessary to form muscles, organs, and tissues, as well as antibodies and enzymes

recombinant DNA DNA that is manipulated to include segments from two or more organisms

retrovirus a virus containing RNA as its genetic material; has the ability to create a "mirror" image in the form of DNA; as RNA is usually created from DNA, this is the reverse, or retro-, process

RFLPs restriction-fragment length polymorphisms; different patterns in the DNA sequence of each person that can be detected by the different fragment lengths of DNA that are produced by cutting DNA with a specific restriction enzyme

ribosome extremely small particle containing ribosomal RNA found in the cytoplasm; the location of protein synthesis

RNA ribonucleic acid; a nucleic acid found in the cytoplasm and also in the nucleus of some cells; one function of RNA is to direct the synthesis of proteins; there are three types of RNA: messenger RNA, ribosomal RNA, and transfer RNA

sex chromosomes chromosome pair 23 in humans; XX in females and XY in males; the X is larger, carrying more genetic information, and, in some cases, genes for sex-linked disorders

sex-linked disorders genetic disorders whose genes are carried on the X chromosome, thus, females are primarily carriers, and the genes for these disorders (e.g., hemophilia, red-green color blindness) are usually only expressed in males

tandem repeats repeated sequences of DNA in the human genome that vary among individuals; can be used as genetic markers

transgenic animals animals that contain genetic information from an animal that is not the donor of either the sperm or ovum; the first living creatures to be patented by the U.S. government

ultrasound examination a prenatal diagnostic test using high-frequency sound waves to perceive and re-create images of a fetus

virus a minute acellular parasite composed of genetic material (either DNA or RNA) and a protein coat, or capsid; not clearly classified as living or nonliving; can only reproduce within living host cells, which they destroy

INDEX

Edward Edelson is science editor of the *New York Daily News* and past president of the National Association of Science Writers. His books include *The ABCs of Prescription Narcotics* and the textbook *Chemical Principles*. He has won awards for his writing from such groups as the American Heart Association, the American Cancer Society, the American Academy of Pediatrics, and the American Psychological Society.

Dale C. Garell, M.D., is medical director of California Children Services, Department of Health Services, County of Los Angeles. He is also associate dean for curriculum at the University of Southern California School of Medicine and clinical professor in the Department of Pediatrics & Family Medicine at the University of Southern California School of Medicine. From 1963 to 1974, he was medical director of the Division of Adolescent Medicine at Children's Hospital in Los Angeles. Dr. Garell has served as president of the Society for Adolescent Medicine, chairman of the youth committee of the American Academy of Pediatrics, and as a forum member of the White House Conference on Children (1970) and White House Conference on Youth (1971). He has also been a member of the editorial board of the *American Journal of Diseases of Children.*

C. Everett Koop, M.D., Sc.D., is former Surgeon General, Deputy Assistant Secretary for Health, and Director of the Office of International Health of the U.S. Public Health Service. A pediatric surgeon with an international reputation, he was previously surgeon-in-chief of Children's Hospital of Philadelphia and professor of pediatric surgery and pediatrics at the University of Pennsylvania. Dr. Koop is the author of more than 175 articles and books on the practice of medicine. He has served as surgery editor of the *Journal of Clinical Pediatrics* and editor-in-chief of the *Journal of Pediatric Surgery*, Dr. Koop has received nine honorary degrees and numerous other awards, including the Denis Brown Gold Medal of the British Association of Paediatric Surgeons, the William E. Ladd Gold Medal of the American Academy of Pediatrics, and the Copernicus Medal of the Surgical Society of Poland. He is a Chevalier of the French Legion of Honor and a member of the Royal College of Surgeons, London.